Tales of a Traveler
in Poetry and Prose

By Author

Brion K Hanks

For information contract:
Brion.Hanks@gmail.com
Brionh502@q.com
My Website: www.BrionKHanks-Poetry.com

Tales of a Traveler
in Poetry and Prose

ISBN: 978-1-963917-24-6 (paperback)
ISBN: 978-1-963917-25-3 (hardback)
ISBN: 978-1-963917-26-0 (ebook)
Library of Congress Control Number: 2024910884

www.GlobalAmbassadorPress.com

PRINTED IN THE UNITED STATES OF AMERICA

Table of Contents

Acknowledgements

I would be remiss if I failed to acknowledge the efforts of my parents, particularly during my early formative years. They taught me to understand that truth matters; that character matters; that family matters; that all lives matter; that being on time matters; that if you choose to do something, be all in with commitment and passion that prevails until the goal(s) is or are achieved. And, as the oldest of five children, to "watch out for your brothers and sisters."

What if this was extended to the entire human family? It's safe to say that our world would be a much better place. If only!

During my human evolution, I have learned that it takes individual effort, our labor, to accomplish anything. And within our sphere of influence, we have but to do what we can, where we can. I suggest, worry not about to what degree but know that you will be helping others through your individual effort.

Several near-death experiences have led me to periodically reflect over subsequent years as to why I remain in human form. Be that as it may, I am grateful for still evolving on this planet. Through my life extension, it remains my intent to always contribute to right human relations. My daily effort advances my spiritual growth along the road before me by living life in a constructive, giving and humane way.

I know that my writing has helped others and has helped me as well. I have sought and received feedback as a means to value human connection and contribution toward right human relations. So, dear reader, my challenge is that you do the same. God knows this world of ours desperately needs it.

Do you want to think on a Universal scale? Do it. I continue to think in that way.

To my wife and long-time friend, Sandra, thank you for being such a great sounding board; providing editorial and honest feedback; and for your enduring love even through health challenges you have experienced. I am a better man for having you in my life.

To my cousin, a Wordsmith in her own right (write), I want to acknowledge her past writing efforts and willingness to review, edit and provide feedback to me during the time of pulling this book together. Thanks for such an awesome effort.

And to my long-time friend, Donna G., who was Donna C. when she was the girl who kissed me in the 5th grade, thanks for caring. After sharing my first book of poetry, *When The Rose Fades*, along with subsequent additional poems, Donna came to appreciate and connect with my writings in ways that demonstrated she really takes the time to think about the poems and prose; provide her thoughts via feedback, and then share with others. And thank you as well for input on this book.

Last, but my no means least, I want to acknowledge my Creator as the First Principle in all things and to convey, as I daily do, that I am grateful for the gift of my life.

Admittedly nowhere near perfect, I remain a work in progress; ever striving to grow my spirit which one day will transition from the seen to the unseen. With that, let us choose light and love to further our efforts for overcoming darkness in all forms. Each of us can be a light shining brighter by the day for truth and freedom. Indeed, *let freedom ring loudly by way of all world people demonstrating right human relations.*

BKH 2021

Preface

I was 23 when I began writing poetry and prose. Those early efforts had to do with life, love and experiences of my youth. Around a dozen or so poems were written but lost or given away, as well as several others during the last 30 years. However, the Universe knows and if any poem was uplifting or helpful to others, I am ok with it.

Still, I continue to write about living life, love, loss, my experiences over many years, and making a difference where I can. My efforts are due in large part to connecting with and relating to those within my sphere of influence. I remain grateful and do feel privileged to have the life I am living.

Wow! Fast forward to 2024. By choice, I have done a great deal of writing during the past three years. The Covid-19 virus, which severally impacted the world in such a tragic and deadly way, caused me to have more time at home because of being restricted regarding public outings as well as my being "retired." This allowed for thoughtful reflection and dreaming on my part. You will see that I have placed dates at the bottom of each poem and prose as a means to timeline my writing.

Notably, in 1984 I moved to Sedona, AZ and worked for an upscale art gallery. During quiet time I would write poems. I found Sedona to be an awe-inspiring location and spiritual in nature as well. Inspiration flowed freely during my year in Sedona. That period of my life, though brief, had a major impact on me and it did so in such a positive way.

Throughout the years that followed I had spurts of writing poetry plus numerous times of writing letters to editors of newspapers in states where I have lived regarding local, state and national issues. Those letters were written in Washington, Colorado, Arizona, Idaho and continue in Oregon.

As a stand-alone portion of this book, I have chosen to include an Essay I began writing in 2008 and which went through several revisions over nearly thirteen years. _**God for an Interim Period of Time**_ is intended to connect heart to heart and spirit to spirit.

After serious reflection upon past world history, the present world travails and the future which does not look too bright, I crafted this Essay and share it with you. It is my hope that you share it as well.

My point is to get people to think! To think about why and what is wrong in this world of ours and get them to understand that positive change can come when the will of the world's peoples is committed to think and act in righteous ways to strengthen right human relations on a global scale.

My writing inspiration comes through meditative thoughts that occur; inner action with people in my life; something seen in nature; a word or phrase heard or sometimes an amazing thought that is like a flash of light. I've even challenged a few people to provide me with three words which I then utilize to create the poem with those three words as the title. A fun thing to do as you have a blank page to create on. As well, fiction is sprinkled amongst my poetry, along with real world experiences.

Because inspiration is so fleeting, when it arrives, I immediately put pen to paper and write down what is flowing in. Thoughts/words can sometimes flow at an amazing pace. A good many of my poems have been initially written in long-hand and done in mere minutes. Thereafter, I type them up and begin a process of editing or "tweaking." I do my wordsmithing until sufficient personal satisfaction is achieved which then frees my mind to move on and stimulate creative juices to craft anew.

I am not a poet looking for fame. Having said that, in my first book of poetry titled: _When The Rose Fades_, I had hundreds of people, both in person and by way of email, contact and thank me or let me know of poems that had special meaning for them. That book of poetry and prose focused on life experience, death and dying, and in particular, Hospice patients/clients, and the effect of loss upon family members and friends left behind.

In 2017 I became a Hospice Volunteer for Partners In Care based out of Bend, Oregon. As of this publication, I was a Hospice Volunteer for six plus years. _When the Rose Fades_ has been made available to Hospice and Home Health workers, volunteers, as well as clients and their family and friends at no charge. _When the Rose Fades_ can be purchased via my website: www.BrionKHanks-Poetry.com.

My website, www.GlobalSafetySuccess.com, was developed for the expressed purpose of bringing to the construction industry, a 272-page book focusing on safety and risk which I co-authored and was published in 2013. The title is: _Safety Under Construction_. After 45+ years of experience in various types of construction, with my last 10 years being a full-time and fiercely dedicated **Project Safety Manager**, plus research that documented thousands of people are killed every year and millions injured on the job, my passion for making a greater safety difference/influence continued by way of this book and was completed following my retirement. It should be noted, I have been talked out of retirement four times to date where I continued as an independent Project Safety Manager.

Back to the book in your hands. The child in each of use has the capacity for profound passion. Whatever our passion of choice is or might be, let us be moved to purposeful, positive action as a means to turn our dreams into reality.

Too many people use the hustle and bustle of life as an excuse for lethargy and lack of action. I invite you to stop and take stock of your life. Meditate in a manner that allows you the chance to genuinely look at what your life has been, what it presently is and what you think it can and hopefully will be? If you conclude that there have been shortfalls in the past, don't be hard on yourself. Since we cannot undue our past, what we have then is the moment...And in the moment is where we have the power to control our actions that build on our future.

The speed of life is so swift! The trials and tribulations on our life journey do impact us in various ways. As I believe in a next life, the short span of our time on this earth is but a prelude to so much more.

The intent of my writings is to induce thought, provide solace, inspire, facilitate forms of closure and help people through whatever may be impacting their life.

With that, it is my hope that people will want to share my writings as a means for them to help others and to help me make a greater difference in this world of ours. It will then do their soul definitive good as well. Giving is such a grand thing that we all should be about!

Do I write for myself? Of course! Sometimes I amaze myself with what is created and which is now on paper. My writing efforts purposely provoke thought as a means to impact our world and the Universe in a positive way. You can as well. It matters not how. What matters is that we choose to do those things that better this desperate world of ours.

I am sure you know that our subconscious is a powerful retainer of what we see, what we hear, what we feel and what we read. Allow it to serve you well because it can.

If you are moved by my writings, and you know of someone that can benefit from reading them, please take the time to share as your way to make a difference in the lives of others. It may be merely one poem, but be sufficiently moved to share it.

Onward and upward is an awesome gift that we have been given. Make the most of it and always remember, tomorrow is a new day! So, I say as one striving spirit, let us all keep on keeping on.

Brion K Hanks 2024

To The Goddess In Thee

You hold a flower in your hands
  And might ponder future plans?
But now, let it be now my love,
  As the sun shines brightly above,
And where nature does abound,
  Listen, listen to every sound.
Believe the scene you do see
  And rejoice in its quiet serenity.
Don't ponder too long about what was
  In order to rise above the world of Uz.
And now, let it be now my love
  As I hand to Thee this dove.
Because you are faithful and kind,
  Do know its happiness we can find.
And if a whisper you should hear,
  'Tis only me wishing you were near!
Should tomorrow be too soon my love,
  Let the goddess in Thee come from above.

BKH 1973

My Friend

Know that I count you as a true friend,
And it is happy memories that you lend.
When I am gone, and if you should yearn,
It is this that I would have you learn:
Quandaries and questions can cause doubt
But problem solving is what life's all about.
It's fine to enjoy happy memories of the past,
If you remember that they fade all too fast.

My friend, life is for us to truly live...
Knowing we gain far more when we give!
Don't hold back...and don't hold still...
For love flows, believe me it really will.
As friendship remains in true spirit,
Please, will you please endear it.

For you my friend, I will always be there
And thus never doubt that I truly care.
So, smile, take one step and then take two,
As I will always wish the best for you!

BKH 1980

The Road Before Me

If I cannot come into this world alone;
If I can't go through life alone;
I know I won't be alone when
It's time to travel from this life.

If I cannot be deserted even when not seen;
If I cannot go unnoticed wherever I am;
I have faith that there is life everlasting.

If I cannot stop a thought once conceived;
If I cannot evade every feeling;
I am convinced my spirit does exist.

If I can accept the road before me;
If "I think and therefore I am;"
I know that "onward and upward" is my path.

If I acknowledge, "To think is to create;"
Then, each day, this traveler will learn
I am enthused by my growing spirit.

And thus, I cherish The Road Before Me!

BKH 1984

What Will You Do Now?

As I lay me down to sleep
A thought occurred to me.
What will you do now?

The full feelings of the flesh
Test this soul thought saved
And cause me to wonder...

Slowly I drifted off to sleep,
And immediately saw myself
In a different kind of dream.

There I was looking into a mirror,
Asking my reflection to speak
About needed understanding.

Guidance was the gift I desired
As I looked into my own eyes
And realized I had changed.

I saw pain which pierced my soul,
As I pondered my purpose in life,
And it produced a new feeling.

I then heard my image softly say,
"You are your own creator,
"And must always seek balance.

"The love that came into your life
"Has truly touched your heart,
"And you now hurt in a new way.

"You've been rocked to your core
"And need to address this question,
"What will you do now?"

My image faded from view
As I heard the echoes,
"What will you do now?
"...Will you do now?
"...Do now?"

BKH 1989

How Long My Love

We've walked and talked and
Loved during the time we had.
It wasn't enough my love.
It just wasn't enough.
As I looked into your eyes,
The tears on your cheeks,
Formed both pain and love.

The connection was magnetic
When first you came into my life.
The ache in my heart has grown,
And now you are gone again.
How long will it be this time?
Bravely, I shout it to the wind
But no answer comes back to me.

A void left at the lake shore;
I wonder, how long my love
Before we might at least
Talk and hold each other?
Painful was this sad parting.
Wherever you might be,
In my heart you will remain.

Now left waiting and wanting,
Still, I will evermore welcome you.
For now, all that I can do is send
Good thoughts and tell you this,
I will always whisper to the wind
That which I whispered to you,
I love you still...I always will.

BKH 1989

I And Thou In Earthly Paradise

When I look into your eyes
I must say, I see paradise.
When I hold you in my arms
I touch paradise.
When your scent is near
I smell paradise.
When your lips touch mine
I taste paradise.
When I make love to Thee
I am in paradise.
Paradise is our striving spirits
Now joined with happy hearts.
Paradise is us together as one.
Yes, I and Thou are paradise!

BKH 1990

Arms Open For You

I open my arms, especially for you.
Come to me, let's see life through.
I'll keep you safe and caress you too.
And will ask God to bless us anew.

Holding you simply feels so good.
I always knew that you understood.
As mates our souls accept our fate.
And know that we can never be late.

Hand in hand we go forward together.
Come what may, fair or foul weather.
Yes, my arms are open just for you,
As we fearlessly seek what is our due.

BKH 1999

You And I Do Make We

Always, you and I do make we.
Together what is it we shall see?
The tide comes in, the tide goes out.
With it, we can release any doubt.
Then this much we surely know
Even our feelings do ebb and flow.

When we reach out to those with a need,
By making a difference, we are in the lead.
Today, tomorrow, and for however long,
Let us journey onward and stay strong.
The deeds we do are the gifts we gained.
Within heart and soul they are ingrained.

Even as you and I do make we,
It is our spirits that remain free.
A spirit young or however old
Accepts the only thing it can hold.
It is the connection to our Creator
That is rightfully down to our core.

BKH 2001

A Quorum of Two

The ultimate Quorum of Two
Is Between Thee and Thy Maker.
Make yourself available today.

When we wander aimlessly through life,
It's due to a loss of focus on the present.
Make yourself available today.

Know that the end of Planet Earth
Is not the end of Thee and me.
Make yourself available today.

Needed is a Quorum of Two
Between Thee and Thy Maker.
Make yourself available today.

Ponder the worth of your own will
And the self-power to succeed.
Make yourself available today.

To experience facing one's fears
Means being fully present.
Make yourself available today.

A Quorum of Two simply requires
Sincere communication with Thy Maker.
Unlimited wisdom is available every day.

BKH 2001

Was Our Best Some Test?

This Earth life raises my spirit
In pursuit of a self-fulfilling future.
While I am, and do remain me,
You are you, but we get to be we.

Even when the moon so full
Wanders amongst the clouds,
Once risen to brighten the night,
We recognize this life so divine.

I wonder, was our best some test,
Where loving a life lived in service
For the greater good could truly
Mean we made a real difference?

The poet writes to express those
Heart-felt words of one seeking
A like-mindedness person who values
The burning desire of a striving spirit.

The veins of life do course within
Those who dare to just be human.
We grow and we go on to that
For which we shall not be denied.

I wonder, was our best some test?
For all we achieved in this lifetime,
No matter what, we do our best
In hopes of leaving a lasting legacy.

BKH 2001

I Love Thee Still

The thought of losing you
Makes me ask, "What will I do?"
How much my heart would ache.
Perhaps it might break?
I love thee still,
And always will.

As you touch the tear upon my cheek
It makes my knees go weak.
My love,oh my dear love,
We fit like hand in glove.
I love thee still,
And always will.

The thought of living without you
Causes me to ask, "Can this be true?"
Hold me closer friend and lover so dear.
We must claim this pain and get clear.
I love thee still,
And always will.

Now, as you quietly lean upon my arm,
Happily, I remain warmed by your charm.
Let us reach to touch our favorite star.
When done together it won't seem so far.
I love thee still,
And always will.

Your future is in your grasp too fast,
But I'll have memories that last and last.
No, no, please not now.
To go on without you, how?
I love thee still,
And always will.

BKH 2003

My Love, My Friend

My love, with you I can happily go on
When we willingly rise to each new dawn.
Life's challenges are before us, we know,
Since it's onward and upward we must go.

When we move patiently as a unit of one
The journey can still relinquish some fun.
Yet, the steady growth we suffer to gain
Sometimes comes from our own pain.

Even still, let us live, laugh and love,
Knowing inspiration comes from above.
My love, my friend, continue at my side.
Do stay the course and relish the ride.

BKH 2003

To The Women I've Loved

Reflection on the past results in memories
Of pleasure, pain and passion aplenty.
Into each other's eyes we would look
Always wanting to see an open book.

Oh how I loved you when once we were young.
As companions on life's journey, even for a little while,
We happily traveled along a lively yet winding road.
We lived, we laughed, and loved as best we could.
Still I wonder and perhaps you do too,
How might our lives have been different...If?

To the women I've loved, listen to this,
I would not have missed what we experienced.
All the pleasure, even the pain which
Helped to mold us into who we became.
Oh for soothe, that river of truth which
We dared to bridge for a moment in time.
Ultimately, we are a product of our time together.

To the women I've loved, please know,
This is not intended as a question of
What might have been...But?
But simply to acknowledge, upon reflection,
That the lessons of life should require our
Effort to do better with each step we take.

To the women I've loved, believe me when I say,
It is my wish that the people we became,
Positively, were helped by being together?
Where I to see you again I would surely say,
"I hope you found love and happiness,
Where you and life were good to each other."

Finally, to the women I've loved,
If the child in me now met the child in thee,
This much I know, I would do better...
Begrudge me not for what might have been,
Since in the end I hope we remain, if only in spirit,
Still friends...This I say to the women I've loved.

BKH 2004

What If There Is No Tomorrow?

I heard a faint whisper on the wind which
Gently caressed my inner being and said,
"Treasure the time you have together."

Perhaps the hardest What If question is,
What if there is no tomorrow?
To be with you then would be enough!

Any sad beginning can be overcome
By every life truly lived to the fullest,
Where love is ushered in from above.

Perhaps the hardest What If question is,
What if there is no tomorrow?
Your hand in my hand would be enough.

Resoundingly we all should know,
The magic is not in memories.
Rather, it's living each special moment.

Perhaps the hardest What If question is,
What if there is no tomorrow?
You in my arms at sunset would be enough.

Woe be unto anyone living in the past,
Where the conclusion drawn is that,
Sadly, such a person has no future.

Perhaps the hardest What If question is,
What if there is no tomorrow?
Loving you for who you are is enough.

The line between pain and pleasure
Is conquered either way because
We know, there needs to be a tomorrow.

Perhaps the hardest What If question is,
What if there is no tomorrow?
Then, together, let us relish today!

BKH 2013

Life Chapters

Unanswered love may live on even when thought lost.
Live another day and another to find the love you deserve.
Blossoms in spring; Daffodils swaying in a gentle breeze and
Sunflowers turn their heads when mesmerized by the sun.
All love, when fresh, has such passion that it wills us forward
Into a future where courage propels us to daily do our part.
When a life chapter closes a new one opens for each of us.
It is in the making that we are found either willing or wanting.
To boldly brave what comes our way today and into the future,
The freedom we have is a gift that shouldn't be squandered.
Since we are stuck with life chapters once they are fully written,
Contribute to a love deluge that can envelope a desperate world.

BKH 2014

Challenge To My Moral Compass

My will was waning because of an alluring smile.
A radiant figure barely seen through a misty fog
Compelled me toward a naked vortex of enchantment.
Was this some sensuous siren sending me a signal?
That would lead to my moral compass' entrapment?

Struggling to avoid such soft wailing I looked away.
But to no avail, enticement propelled me forward.
Could the loss of my moral compass now result in
Giving way to intense and uncontrollable passion?
I knew not how to think about this or even respond.

Pleasured like never before, and completely spent,
All I could do was quietly watch the siren drift away,
As I tried to understand what had just happened?
Was I still in this world when seduced in such a way
Which resulted in questioning my moral compass?

Oh, the wound of wild yet willing pleasure so peculiar.
Was this angelic or carnal casting of such a spell
That caused me to be sucked into a tidal whirlpool?
Could there be any escape worthy of raising myself up
To live beyond such an encounter here on earth?
　　　I was left to wonder?

BKH 2019

Random, Real Or Some Illusion

What kind of fun under the sun was this?
Knowing passion never goes out of fashion,
Was this random, real or some illusion?

With eyes expressing hunger for each other,
Was this some illicit life episode that occurred?
And was past passion percolating into our now?

Even in the moonlight there was skinny dipping.
Eagerness for pleasure without any distraction;
Whether nighttime or daytime, it didn't matter.

Who shouted first for a titillating youth pill?
There had been no time even for infatuation.
Was this random, real or some illusion?

During this marathon of arrogant love making,
Did we go crazy with such conscious craving?
Was there any purpose to such a coupling?

Neither wanted such novelty to ever wear off.
Yet, what was left unsaid as one walked away?
In parting, our eyes said what we couldn't say.

Why then did one decide to vanish so soon?
There was absolutely no humor in a rumor.
Had it been random, real or some illusion?

BKH 2020

The Past, Present And Future

What if you had pursued the person
   Who first kissed you? What If?
What if you had chosen to turn right
   Instead of left and met a different "soul mate?"
Be not haunted by what might have been?
   Would you; could you; should you do the
Things you did not do a long time ago?
   Who's in control of your happiness today?
Life choices need not have haunting voices.
   Thinking about what might have been
Will not change the life you've lived to date.
   I have met regret and it got me nowhere.

Normalcy, whatever that is known to be,
   Does not have to be a lifetime nemesis.
The magic of motivation is you get to choose.
   Wishing cannot change one iota of the past.
Today, make every precious moment count.
   A life vocation is service for the life-stream.
Treasure the closeness of family and friends.
   Never allow emptiness to creep into your life.
What might have been is for those who wonder,
   And are stuck living in an unchangeable past.
A wise you puts aside what might have been;
   Believes in now, and builds upon your future.
I have to ask, why wouldn't you?

BKH 2020

Was It Over?

Reluctantly we met by the lake shore.
With heartache, I looked into your eyes.
Such sadness hung on the two of us.
I asked, "What happened and is it over?"
Years flashed by as memories surfaced
Only to intensify the immediate pain that
Was rapidly welling up on this sad day.
You, who had declared your love first,
Stood on the precipice of walking away.
Two extremely independent people
Couldn't or wouldn't put pride aside.
Such aching was baking in the sun as
I placed a tender kiss on your cheek.
I wondered how will we be happy now?
My wistfulness was for all the right reasons.

Can denial, plus distance, now nullify love?
Tears on your cheeks, as you turned first,
Fell with each departing step you took.
I sunk to a new low as you walked away.
Now separated with life passion denied,
It occurred to me that two as one can
Overcome what had senselessly torn us apart.
Lonely weeks had slipped painfully away when
An unexpected incident drew us back together.
The result became the launch of a new beginning
Which allowed for our flourishing long-term union.
A commitment to mutually resolve life challenges
Has been instrumental for our relationship's survival.
Years of gratitude fortifying our love does continue
And has held up because we knew, it could not be over.

BKH 2021

31

Soul Mates

Somehow, once when we first met,
There was such a sense of connecion.
Many have said, "I met my soul mate."
At a minimum for me I met my mate
With whom our souls are so aligned.
To beat back the darkness and
Remain always true to ourselves,
We are guided by a lighthouse beacon.
Each day we read each other's minds
And 99% of the time we are in tune.
The home we have in each other's heart
Allows us to breathe life for the Universe.
The probability of getting to a perfect match
Should never be allowed to hold us back.

BKH 2021

Someone Lonely On A Sunny Day

Today you choose rare passion for fun.
Stay or go, tell me are you on the run?
Waning proof by the starry moonlight,
Was lust leaving in a state of lonely fright?
We know a flower lost its bloom today.
As the sun rose, what do you now say?

I leaned in to try and slow your pace,
Yet you chose to quickly join some race.
I am left wondering if you will be alright?
And to sadly watch you wander out of sight.
The cause of pleasure has sped away
When I was softly asking you to stay.

What was it that you hoped to teach me,
As someone found lonely under that tree?
Embraces voided, what can happen now?
Did you stew over the why or even the how?
Seemingly selfish intent by one who would dare
Leave on an unknown road with nary a care.

Under the pretext of needing a fresh start,
Someone lonely on a sunny day did depart.
It is a sad fact that you would not even try,
As I wonder are you truly saying goodbye?
When you left shouting, "I deserve my due,"
How will I remember the spirited side of you?

BKH 2020

Stars At The Sea Shore

Dare I say, it was a dream come true
When seeing that it turned out to be you.
I felt blessed that we found each other
On this Earth which we call our Mother.

Hand in hand we walked along the shore.
Pleased yet hoping for so much more.
As I whispered sweet nothings in your ear
You leaned in to say what I wanted to hear.

What is this feeling that stirs, my new friend,
As I yearn for more of you that won't end?
Such a new closeness which feels so good
Was heartfelt magnetism and being understood.

Dogs running free and children at play
Is beach perfect on such a glorious day.
Wind and waves trigger the salty air
As we both commit to being fully fair.

With a desire for coincidence to slip away,
Let us wish for no end to this remarkable day.
Nearness and a need to not be done yet,
Together we treasured an awesome sunset.

It is in knowing tomorrow will be a new day,
And with our combined effort all can be okay.
To give in to this raw and real yearning
Means we can experience a rare burning.

It is such wonder materializing on this day
Begetting shared passion and purpose, I pray.
We are destined now for a life to boldly live,
Knowing we gain far more when we give.

What are newfound friends now for
If not to recognize neither is a bore.
And with a fierce determination to be true,
Let's put aside what ifs and allow our due.

BKH 2020

Do We Get Over Lost Love?

Why did "things" have to end so bad?
How long should we have to be sad?
Days slip away but not the memories,
And it does no good to change countries.
Weeks turn into months, and then years.
Will tears wash away any present fears?
Do we get over lost love even today?
Can we move beyond memories that stay?
What ifs can't change or remove our past.
Let us remember, it's only now that does last.
Even if we barter for history to be rewritten
It won't change with whom we were smitten.
It can't be wrong to remove a loss love dam,
Even when it might flow and then go, wham!
But we continue on with our separate lives
And have been busy like many beehives.
Come what may, those standing by us today
Count the most and do rise above the fray.
Letting go of the past is moving on now
And never fearing the why or even the how.

BKH 2021

For The Love Of You

So captivated was I the first time I saw you.
Could thoughts materialize into my action
As a means for me to know you like no other?
Feeling a magnetic pull, you tugged at my heart.
Can days, weeks and months turn into years
If life's journey is joined because of our union?
I craved to grow this thrilling thing called love.
Absorbed by a rare passion, even to this day,
Grateful am I for the seasons we can share.
Never enough, and only for the love of you,
I remain captivated by the aura of you in totality.

In constant bloom, love will find ways for
Our choosing to always support each other.
Living through times of tears or even fears
Can be overcome by the love we boldly share.
To live on, growing through our undying love,
Let's be grateful for our having found each other.
To endure, yet enjoy the thrilling speed of life,
May we always recognize the best in each other
As we weather any storms that come our way.
Accepting each other as equals grows togetherness.
Sincerely I do, and only for the love of you.

BKH 2021

Love Missed

Listen! Are you listening?
Oh babe, just maybe
It was me that missed you more.
So long ago, we had our way
When once we were known as us.
Was it only pretending, this young love?

Oh babe, just maybe
We should find each other again and
Give two a chance to become one?
I would have you know this grownup child
Has put down the me who once was wild.

Oh babe, just maybe
To believe love lives in each other still,
And that we have but to realize it,
Only requires us to voice our choice
And then reach out for each other today.

Oh babe, just maybe
We go from doubt to love done right.
Strike one wasn't fun and two won't do.
Don't put one foot out the door and
Allow strike three to deny a deserving us.
Oh babe, just maybe

Our wavelengths can finally be one.
To face the chase and never fear freedom,
We can rejoice in our parallel path?
If we now choose to patiently work at it,
Our love unison will be a journey so long.

BKH 2021

We Lean On Each Other

The Winds of change swiftly pushed us
Toward what became our collision course.
At first knowing nothing about each other,
Yet sensing there really was something,
We quietly grew to crave each other.
Still, years slipped slowly away before
Our music quenched pent-up yearning.
Once caught, we couldn't be torn apart.
Feeling the pain that at times touched you,
I pulled you in and softly said, "Lean on me."
Our senses so in tune and easily meshed,
Eased us into a life of profound togetherness.

Shock came by learning one could too soon
Be gone when we thought we were forever.
Now, for however long, we lean on each other.
Better are we for our combined efforts and
Caring enough to be committed help-mates.
Shared tales and trails were ours for awhile.
At this time, pursuit of another beginning
Hopefully is to further our cherished world?
While darkness dares to descend upon us,
We will remain positive and open to the light.
Our leap of faith resulted in finding each other.
God willing, we will continue to lean on each other.

BKH 2020

A Time For Greater Love

Is it not a time for greater love?
Is love not a worthy contribution
To the soul of this world of ours?

When it comes to love, be not lazy.
To promote love and good living
Is to beget the reward of happiness.

Right action will be driven by love.
Give me your hand and get my heart
As we listen to voices that give choices.

By shunning enemies of love and light,
And being renowned for growing love,
We will surely affect positive change.

As a promoter who expands love,
Fear not feedback while living life.
A glowing reward will be love realized.

Any and all failures can be overcome
When selfless expression dares feed,
and bravely fuel, the fire of greater love.

Love provides a rock-solid foundation
Upon which to inspire and be inspired by.
Surely, now is the time for greater love.

BKH 2020

A Love Song

I wonder, why would you walk away
When I would have met you half way?
Parting so painful have I come to know,
As you are hell bent to suddenly go.

A new option was to be yours today.
What's that I think I heard you say?
Yes, yes! You know I love you too,
As I sing a love song just for you.
Lamenting passion of new found love
Was delivered by a precious dove.

Today, there can be no pretending
When you can have love unending.
After all, neither of us is at all shy.
As I'm left to sort out the truth or a lie.
The ambrosia of you is fading away
And no longer will I ask you to stay.

Of each other, we did not get our fill.
I wonder, can we love each other still?
You have wandered off and for what;
To sever love by a door you shut?
What is going to be your certain cost
For this love that you have lost?

Now missing is a mountain of love,
After thinking we did fit like a glove.
My awe fades for a love gone wrong
As I reach the end of this love song.

BKH 2020

Turn Back The Clock

What if mistakes were made in this life?
Still, we cannot turn back the clock,
Nor live on what might have been.
We can love and hope to be loved.
And with purpose, pursue what can be.
Yet, be not dazed by failure or farewells.

We can care for those less fortunate.
Know that doing nothing is harmful.
Of bygone times, what was left unsaid?
Ok, ask, have we been true to ourselves?
Truth to power requires that we speak up.
And righteous indignation needs free will.

Self-awareness is to be ever attentive.
Let reason prevail as our solemn duty.
Foremost, let us pursue spiritual growth.
You know we cannot turn back the clock.
So, let us live to increase light and love.
Then might we know heaven on earth.

BKH 2020

The Window

Trinkets sitting on a window sill
Are there by virtue of our free will.
Beyond that window we can see
All that can virtually set us free.
Once when looking in I saw you
And knew love is ours to pursue.
Through this window, even at night,
Does provide for a wonderful sight.
For us, don't give up and don't give in
Afterall, looking out or in isn't a sin.

When looking out watch for trolls
Who are in pursuit of lonely souls.
I will insulate you against any evil
Or any hounding human boll weevil.
Think big, if thinking about tomorrow,
And never be paralyzed by any sorrow.
Allow me to give you a gentle shove
As a window is not a barricade to love.
Hold on to hope and never despair
As I am always there and truly care.

BKH 2021

Who Is Left To Tell I Love You?

We rent our physical body for awhile.
The length of time is our own "trial."
Once our earthly deeds are done
It's time to experience a setting sun.

Believe not that any death is a day of doom.
Rather, believe it is truly a day to bloom.
What is coming is but a great adventure
With a budding spirit as your treasure.

Now, who is left to tell I love you?
Relief is yours when you see this through.
By resolving what is your true identity
You will arrive at selfless serenity.

The greatest yet stunning gift, your soul,
Now requires that you do take control.
You are off in pursuit of eternity today,
And have only to allow come what may.

Freely embrace the transition you will feel,
Because your soul already sealed the deal.
Now you are needed fully in that moment.
Acceptance is daring to now be content.

After all, it shall be your royal due
And you need simply to continue.
Again, who is left to tell I love you?
You know we need to hear it too.

BKH 2001

What If There Is No Tomorrow?

I heard a faint whisper on the wind which
Gently caressed my inner being and said,
"Treasure the time you have together."

Perhaps the hardest What If question is,
What if there is no tomorrow?
To be with you then would be enough!

Any sad beginning can be overcome
By every life truly lived to the fullest,
Where love is ushered in from above.

Perhaps the hardest What If question is,
What if there is no tomorrow?
Your hand in my hand would be enough.

Resoundingly we all should know,
The magic is not in memories.
Rather, it's living each special moment.

Perhaps the hardest What If question is,
What if there is no tomorrow?
You in my arms at sunset would be enough.

Woe be unto anyone living in the past,
Where the conclusion drawn is that,
Sadly, such a person has no future.

Perhaps the hardest What If question is,
What if there is no tomorrow?
Loving you for who you are is enough.

The line between pain and pleasure
Is conquered either way because
We know, there needs to be a tomorrow.

Perhaps the hardest What If question is,
What if there is no tomorrow?
Then, together, let us relish today!

BKH 2013

One Transition

Though I now look upon the old you
And feel an immediate sense of loss,
I realize the future must now
Command your spirit's utmost attention.
Day by day, until we meet again,
Search that great vastness
With courage and determination.
We must believe you will be all right.
After all, this is something each of us must do.
Though you have now gone ahead,
One day I will catch up and embrace
The new you and I will know then
That life really does go on...
Should you check back now and then,
I hope you find me with a smile
Upon my face and happiness
In my heart...seeking light and
Love as the path to a brighter future.
Remember, with beauty and balance as
Your armor, you will be blessed by rapid growth.
Farewell dear friend...God's speed.

BKH 1982

This poem was written by Brion after the sudden loss of his Uncle Gene.
It is the first poem he wrote regarding losing a family member or friend.
It would not be the last.

Beginning Anew

With the death of a family member or friend,
I am comforted in knowing it isn't the end.
Afterall, it is our individual birth
That comes upon leaving this Earth.
For those of us who now remain
There is an understandable, intense pain.
Our wonderings as to why
Will eventually lead to less and less cries.
Memories of our loved one can
Lend us strength for the day we must stand
At the door to the heavenly beyond,
Looking for a smile when we are gone.
There can be no fear when we have faith
Because angels of light shall keep us safe.
It is then, in beginning anew,
To our family member or friend,
We must now bid a fond ado...
As our Creator is not done with me or you.

BKH 1982

An End Is Only Another Beginning

Go and give yourself the grand gift.
Do so now before the Earth does drift.
Dare to feel free and face your fears,
By moving beyond any pain of past years.
You are your own champion today and tomorrow.
Now forgive yourself and release any sorrow.

Be relieved and know you are not late
And that this journey has been worth the wait.
Sing a song of hope so all shall see,
Beginning is to be set free.
Focus on the future and stay the course.
If you should look back, have no remorse.

Don't point a finger or cast blame
Because life, you know, is not a game.
Get this, as human beings we should
Do rather than say we could.
The secret of our Creator's sharing,
Child of the ages, is genuine caring.

Moving on past the start
Is accomplished by your heroic heart.
The world beyond, my dear friend,
Once believe in, gets you past this end.
Memories remain after you are gone,
As the spirit within thee ventures on.

BKH 1984

Let Me Fear Not Forever

Let me fear not forever
As I journey on and on.

I accept that tomorrow requires
Leaving yesterday and today.
Truly, this grand gift of life deserves
My full attention and intention.

Let me fear not forever
As I journey on and on.

The test of my spirit is found
Both in this moment and in time.
Always shall I strive at growing,
As unconditional love precedes my labor.

And so, let me fear not forever
As I journey on and on.

BKH 1984

Traveler Of The Universe

The Universal Bow does know
That you, as an arrow,
Can fly straight and narrow.

As a traveler of the grand Universe,
You will be tested from time to time
Upon the ladder of life you must climb.

When you see your way is clear,
Take faith as your true friend,
For its comfort will be a godsend.

Then with our prayers behind you
Go forth, but with careful speed,
And take responsibility while in the lead.

Oh traveler, you have the Universe
And the time to know the unknown,
While demonstrating daily how you have grown.

Don't hurry, it is not a race.
Do pace your travels and in time
Taller mountains you will climb.

Today you see the horizon as tomorrow.
If memories were moments along the way,
Then goals shall become deeds, day by day.

Oh traveler, now you do have vision.
So set your sights on high,
And remember, this is not goodbye...

BKH 1984

Earthling For Now

Who has not wondered why they are here?
Certainly, I have!
I wondered in my infancy; I wondered
More in my adolescence.
Now, I wonder most as an adult who
Seeks to understand my reason for being?

Is Earth some great big laboratory,
Like a fish bowl, for all to see?
Are we Earthlings watched from afar
And manipulated without our knowledge?
I am an Earthling for now, but no one has
The right to tamper with my being!
I am a free moral agent who understands
Accountability and responsibility!

Yes, I am an Earthling for now...and
I know that I have lessons to learn.
I ask that no one come near me in disguise.
Do not divide the wisdom I seek.
Do not hide the reason for my being.
I will search it out and come to know why.

One day I will no longer be an Earthling.
And then, in moving onward and upward,
As a traveler of the Universe, I will
Seek out you Gods and Goddesses
And ask the reason for your being, that
I may then better understand my own?
Know that I am coming; know that I dare
To ask questions and will expect answers!

BKH 1989

A Journey

A journey filled with
 Hopes and dreams,
Just to get started,
 Surely means
We must risk stepping out
 On the path right now.
And through our inner faith,
 Never fearing why or how.

With a love for living
 Fully each and every day,
Be about taking that risk
 Come what may.
A journey needs genius
 From both you and me.
And that we look beyond
 Any horizon we shall see.

When freedom and being fearless
 Are clearly taken to heart,
I must ask myself and you today,
 Is now too soon to start?
Oh, to be a part of something
 Much bigger than we are,
And to journey safely beyond
 The stars viewed afar.

Let us not beat up ourselves
 About anything in the past,
For a journey takes us to
 A future that will last.
At this moment in time
 The step we take first,
Puts us on our way to where
 Only steps quench our thirst.

The journey is worth it when
 We know there is no end,
But requires stepping on the path
 And to hopefully take a friend.
So, be bold, be brave and
 Be about fulfilling needs
Today, tomorrow and always
 Journey onward and plant seeds.

BKH 1997

51

Gone In Search Of More

In our memory now you stand
As we struggle to understand.
Oh, how we do painfully grieve
The fact that you must leave.

It is your smile we shall always see,
That now allows us to set you free.
May the connection to God guide you
And help us through our pain too.

You are fetched to heaven we know
As your guardian angel tells us so.
Take heart oh father and friend
As we carry on until our own end.

Please be angel when you can
As we loved more than just the man.
You've gone ahead to see the place
And we must believe it's not a race.

Even as we try to work out the why,
These are tears of joy we now cry.
Be brave dear father and friend,
As our hearts take time to mend.

BKH 1999

Soon I Will

Soon I will travel at the speed of light.
A tremendous journey, not a plight.
Soon I will see those who've gone before.
And then travel on to see so much more.

Soon I will be an angel on high.
To get there I realize I must die.
In my mind, on this, I shall be clear
As the end of my earthly life draws near.

Soon I will experience my soul being set free,
Like a butterfly, even still, I will be me.
Soon I will go from the seen to the unseen
And shall discover this reality is not a dream.

Soon I will feel my heartbeat cease.
I am ready for my soul's release
For it is with this gift so grand
I shall take the Great Hand.

Soon I will sow immense, unconditional love
By watching over each precious dove.
Soon I will accept my moment to depart,
Because I know it's simply my new start.

BKH 2000

Brion wrote this poem for and to honor Dr. Elisabeth Kubler-Ross who pioneered and helped to bring Hospice to the United States. In 2000, Brion and his friend, Rich Carpenter, met with Elisabeth at her home in Arizona, two days in a row, to discuss death and dying and their poetry book, *When The Rose Fades*. Elisabeth agreed to and did write the Introduction for their book. This book can be purchased Elisabeth agreed to and did write the Introduction for their book. This book can be purchased by going to Brion's website: www.GlobalSafetySuccess.com. Click on "Other Writings" to review and purchase that poetry book; or purchase it at *www.BrionKHanks-Poetry.com.*

After Brion's brother, Geoff, died in 1989, his Mom became a Hospice Volunteer and found it rewarding. Subsequent to retiring, in 2017 Brion became a Hospice Volunteer with Partners In Care based out of Bend, OR. His book of poetry, entitled *When The Rose Fades* has been shared with clients and their family and friends with the intent to help in every way possible...

When My Rose Fades

Oh, how I watched thee grow and bloom
My sweet, sweet love.
Now you won't leave your room
And choose to live like a lonely dove.

How we laughed, loved and lived life so full.
For years we were a great unit of one.
Yet, now you feel and alluring unseen pull
And sense your life is now done.

If it's true, be not afraid of tomorrow
My sweet, sweet love.
Even when I feel such sad, sad sorrow,
It was because we do fit like a glove.

You say, "When my rose fades it means
I am choosing my moment to go."
If it must be, then fulfill your dreams
As you take my heart in tow.

Yet, I would bargain my soul
And the devil be damned
If I could keep you whole
And soft like a newborn lamb.

Oh how I love Thee still, and always will
My sweet, sweet love.
Of you I could never get my fill,
Even as you are hastened from above.

I love Thee still, and always will
My sweet, sweet love.
I love Thee still, and always will (fading out),
Oh, how I love Thee still my sweet, sweet love.

BKH 2019

A Signal To Find My Way

What comes of life,
This great and grand blur,
That beats and hums and purrs.

My memory of you is found
In this rose so white
That brightens even the darkest night.

Moonlight on the water
Oh how it can charm,
And now my heart it must warm.

Such parting was not our plan
When we loved each other so.
I miss you; I miss you please know.

My mind still reels as I must ask,
Where have you gone this day?
Send me a signal so I'll find my way.

BKH 2000

In Search Of Self

In search of self is a daily prayer.
Now know your life was not an error.
Though you may not pass this way again
Please anticipate what it is you win!
When you cast off the chains of old
You will be such a sight to behold.
Beloved, do not be controlled by fear
As you begin your voyage from here.
With the genesis of a brave and beautiful you
We are comforted knowing you'll make it through.
As family and friends consent, they must know,
One's acceptance means it's your time to go.
So, in search of self does surely mean,
You're off to pursue a much bigger dream.

BKH 2000

Was I Dreaming?

I saw myself sitting on a large rock
Looking down upon people watching a scene.
It was strange how no one seemed to see me.
Yet all my senses were working perfectly!
What was happening to me?

I was there and everything seemed real.
When I thought of walking on an ocean shore,
In a flash I was there on the beach.
I could hear it, smell it, and feel it too.
What was happening to me?

I said to a man walking by,
"Can you see me? Can you hear me?"
He just kept walking as if I was not there.
I said, "There's something strange going on."
What was happening to me?

Then I thought of talking to my Mom.
And in a flash, I was in her living room.
She was sitting with a friend and both were crying.
I said, "Mom, what's the matter?"
As if I was not there, my Mom said to her friend,
"My son was far too young."
Without even thinking I said out loud,
"What do you mean, I'm right here!"
They did not see me, but I was there!
What was happening to me?

Still crying, my Mom's friend said,
"Drunk drivers seem to always walk away."
Then in a flash I was at the scene of an accident.
They were covering my lifeless body.
I thought, how can this be?
I can't be dead when I know I am alive!
What happened to me?

Was I dreaming?
Can two worlds be so real?
I had no pain or limitations.
This can't be so?
It can't be, can it?
Was I dreaming?

BKH 2000

You By The Sea

Allow yourself to be
Curious yet calm by the sea.
Now hear each ocean wave
Caress the cliff and secret cave.
Breathe deep and smell the salty air.
For you, in this moment, it is so fair.
You are able to accept even this now,
Having lost no sleep over the why or how.

Where the sea meets you and the land,
Believe you can bravely rise to stand.
Visualize your wings at the ready
As you prepare to leave the jetty.
Your guardian angel at your side
Declares you have nothing to hide.

Now it's up, up and away,
As you begin a new life today.
Don't be afraid to look down
But do believe in what you have found.
For now, we accept being left behind,
And can, knowing its happiness you will find.

BKH 2000

A Piece Of Heaven

If the past cannot be changed,
Then the future must be made.
Issues resolved while here on Earth
Clear the way for rapid, unseen growth.
The lightness of sprit does mean
One is above and beyond us now.
It's no trick this trade that was made.
For a leap of faith shall give freedom
To enjoy the new life that comes next.
A piece of heaven is ours to share.
So, take your place and always care.
Be in the moment, and adjust we must
To the change that comes for us all.

BKH 2001

No Greater Gift Can I Now Have

This call to action does require that I
Accept, and relish my own transition.
No greater gift can I now have than
To know mortal becomes immortal.

More than once, it has been said to me,
"Nothing is gained from asking why?"
How easy to say but hard to elude.

Some may wonder if life goes on?
Indeed, there is no danger in death.
As well, there is no need for fear.

This earthly time I've gratefully had
Came to be a grand spiritual journey.
I will be fulfilled through contributing
To the betterment of humanity and myself.

I accept my record which has been written.
Now, with whatever time I have left,
I intend to live mainly in the moment
In order to really make the most of it.

I admit, I am not a prisoner in my body.
Rather, I have a soul with a beautiful exterior.
The joy of the journey should surely be
My spirit is aware and resolved to moving on.

No greater gift have I come to realize, and
Happily accept, is that mortal becomes immortal.
This brief time here on Planet Earth shall be
Exchanged for a spiritual expedition I earned.

BKH 2001

There Comes A Time

There comes a time
For each, the ultimate day.
Some are surprised
When it's time to slip away.

Even as it shall arrive,
None need declare a truce.
To confidently stay the course
Means never say, "What's the use?"

Oh, how we might want to create
Time that would stand still.
So that we could get a
Lingering amount of life's fill.

There comes a time,
In fact, for everyone.
To acknowledge this gift
And accept this life is done.

Look out, look up and listen too,
As you hold all within your heart.
Never doubt such a glorious day
That bestows this certain new start.

Acceptance does not mean
You are giving up at all.
As should be, in true spirit,
You've simply heard your call.

We know, there comes a time
To cast off each Earthly chain.
Whether it is to rise or fall,
Each of us gets to explain.

We shall see the other side
When once we do let go.
And from there our spark
Is off to earn its greater glow.

BKH 2001

Just One Day

Yonder stands a mountain so grand.
Majestic in its state until it is no more.
Just one day provides all that I see
And allows me to feel alive, oh so alive!

With each breath that I confidently take
I can and do choose to make the most of it.
Acceptance now so serene releases my
Spirit to feel rewarded, oh so rewarded.

I realize, in this precious moment, that
Just one day must be the focus for me.
I will love always and happily live forever
Even in the unseen, oh the great unseen.

To know that you must surely carry on
Enables me to suffer this present pain.
I can go through the process because
Of my strong faith, oh my undying faith.

Lift yourself up and rejoice with my choice.
Just one day of seeing your smiling face
Gives me such comfort and the courage
To carry on, oh the courage to carry on.

The stopover on Earth, even for awhile,
Has been a great and rewarding privilege.
My purpose for living is to make a difference
Today and thereafter, oh the thereafter.

BKH 2001

In Fate's Grip

What thinking actually takes place
When you are found in fate's grip?
Is it fear or faith seen on your face,
As you arrive at the end of this trip?

Even so, you cannot be late
When on your way to forever.
My dear, dear one, fear not your fate
As you press on with each endeavor.

Since there is no great mystery
Regarding all that you have done,
Each future becomes your history.
So, never feel the need to be on the run.

As you are mindful of the greater good,
It's time to rise up and begin your next trip.
Our relief is in knowing you understood,
As you accept your journey in fate's grip.

BKH 2002

A Cherub Left Too Soon

Our Arms do ache for Thee
Since you left our family tree.
A Cherub you shall surely be
Only to remain in our memory.

You are gone and we softly cry,
Even as we quietly ask, "Why?"
For no lack of unconditional love,
Still, you left like a resolute dove.

Such a passing has no bright side
And our feelings we shall not hide.
This painful loss we know and feel
Cannot be something soon to heal.

Even before a deserved Earthly start
We suffer the fact that you did depart.
On a journey that came much too soon,
You depart and travel beyond our moon.

From the seen, yet ushered to the unseen,
Dare to mold and grow your soul so clean.
Your loss we must acknowledge and endure
Knowing our earthly experience ends for sure.

BKH 2002

Wait For Me

When the wind stopped, and all was still,
I was startled to hear you say, "Wait for me!"
Your wailing words fully washed over me.
When I left you for another realm, my dear,
It was too late to wait, too late to change.
The dye was cast and death snared me.
I see the other side and must confess,
It's much like it is where you now remain.

Fear not what you cannot see, my dear.
There is no need to cry out, "Wait for me!"
Our time traveled together was wonderful.
Rejoice through memories but do let me go.
Soon enough we shall see each other again.
Until that time, I shall happily watch over Thee.
Now hear this from your angel, my good friend,
The journey has just begun...yes, just begun.
I will, in the next realm, patiently wait for you.

The school called life spearheads us forward.
Yet, no crystal ball can show the exact way
But be convinced that we can make the most
Of everything ahead of our fearless spirits.
We go and grow the seeds we need to sow.
Today cannot hold back what is tomorrow.
Just as tomorrow cannot hold back the future.
The path that is onward and upward turns
Even when you would have it do otherwise.
To live and learn means, simply, live and learn.
Now I'm off to do exactly that my dear friend.
When it's your time do join me on the journey.

BKH 2002

We Must Go Through It

Lives saddened by the shock
Of learning what is drawing near
Does leave such pain in its wake.

We know what will happen
But what does it ultimately mean?
Would that it could be a dream.

A full life missed here on Earth
Is exchanged for life everlasting.
Put bluntly, we must go through it.

Even mixed emotions cannot
Be changed by some potion
Or the casting of a hollow spell.

Was it that you received
Heaven's direct mail and now
Need preparation for setting sail?

For each and every one of us,
In order to get to the other side,
We must, and shall, go through it.

BKH 2002

Dream Or Do

Dream or do?
It's true for me and you!
If one dares to explore
One cannot be a bore.

It is the song within your soul
That helps to keep you whole.
You can tell yourself this,
In the next life will be bliss.

Dream or do?
Leaves a choice to be blue.
Or you can accept this hand
And proceed with your plan.

As moonbeams circle us tonight
Hold me close before taking flight.
I am warmed as you tickle me so.
How it will hurt when I must let you go.

Dream or do?
Now or later, you have the clue.
Give thanks for this distance run,
And know your journey is not done.

Thank you for being my friend,
And do believe this is not the end.
Imagine the essence of my heart in tow,
And then simply choose to make it so.

BKH 2002

Hold On

I went to the depths of
Deep, dark despair and
Managed to hold on.

A strong feeling urged me
To jump overboard but
I was able to hold on.

When I was drowning,
And fighting for my life,
I heard, "Hold on!"

Where the sea met the shore
I quietly cried out for help
And again heard, "Hold on."

At death's door, and not
Wanting to go through it,
Still I heard, "Hold on."

Then someone cried out,
"I don't want to live..."
And I heard myself say,
"Hold on!"

Even in "a million little pieces,"
When all seems so hopeless,
We must hold on.

Always, it is our inner spirit
That truly knows we can
Hold on.

Choose to embrace this counsel.
Tomorrow arrives as a new day.
So, hold on, and bravely carry on!

BKH 2003

Through A Child's Eyes

"Did the Pied Piper lead my Mommy away?
"Why did my Mommy die?
"Is my Mommy in heaven?
"Did I do something wrong?
"Is it because she doesn't love me anymore?
"If I promise to be good forever, will my Mommy come back?
"Can my Mommy ever come back to me?
"Will I see my Mommy again?
"Is my Daddy going to die and leave me alone?
"Am I going to die too?
"Why does God take people away?
"Where does everyone go when they die?
"I don't understand...

"Hey God, are you listening?"
Jimmy did not hear a sound as he sat under a tree in the park.
Looking so sad, he then said, "Is anybody listening?"
The breeze made the leaves rustle on the tree Jimmy sat under.
Then he heard, "Jimmy, look up here."
Sitting on a limb was a smiling young boy with a glow all around him.
"My name is Tim and God asked me to talk with you."
"Thank you," said Jimmy. "I was feeling so alone."
Tim said, "I am an angel and I'm here to tell you something.
"You have been a good boy and you have done nothing wrong.
"Your Mommy is ok and sends her love to you. She asked me to
"Tell you that she loves you very much and that she will see you again,
"But you have to grow and learn about life on Earth. She says that
"Your Daddy will be with you so don't be afraid. Your Mommy wants
"You to grow up and become a good man and make a difference
"With your life. Will you do that?"

"Yes!" Jimmy said. And then he asked, "Do you think I can
"Talk to my Mommy?" Tim said, "Sure, you can talk to your Mommy
"Anytime you want. She hears you and said for you to know that
"She is around you but you can't see her, that's all...and for you to
"Remember, there's nothing to be afraid of, you will be fine."

Jimmy said, "Thanks for talking with me Tim. I feel better. I'm going to
Go and play with my friends now."
Tim said, "You're welcome Jimmy. Have a good time and be careful."

Ok!" Jimmy said as he ran off to play.

BKH 2003

Your Ship Set Sail

I know your ship is about to set sail.
Once aboard, know you did not fail.
Steadily, your ship shall catch the tide,
As you realize there's nothing to hide.
You are headed out to that grand sea,
Which means you have been set free.

Off you go my brave and loving friend,
Remember to be patient while on the mend.
You are about to experience something great
And should appreciate you are not late,
Since it was you who selected this date.
Our love and praise will carry you though.
Now accept what you have chosen to do.

If we cannot change even this day,
What more is there that we can say?
By choice, your ship has now set sail.
So please leave signs that pierce the veil.
Keep us within sight and in your mind,
After all, we shall not be far behind.

BKH 2003

The Sun That Sets

I loved Thee from the start
When first our eyes did meet.
Such passion that set us apart
Causes me to know it was a treat.

To embrace this kind of caring,
Is the sun rising or has the sun set?
Yet there is pain that's tearing
At my heart where you are kept.

I cry out in hopes it is not true
Yet know you've gone from view.
How long might I be blue
As I ponder letting go of you?

While we come and then we go,
The time in between seems so short.
Now you take my heart in tow
Until the next time we might court.

The sun sets I am sad to say
While I seek to understand.
Even though you've left today
I'm now stuck on this lonely land.

Yet, can I see your beautiful smile
And subtle grin I came to know.
Now I must be alone for awhile
Until my guardian angel says, "Let's go."

BKH 2004

This Is My Life

I am not today
Who I was yesterday.
I am today not
Who I'll be tomorrow.
Even so, there is no sorrow.

This is my life,
Even filled often with strife.
This is my life
That enjoys the reward of reason.
Happily, it is mine in every season.

To learn from one's past
Needs action taken so fast.
Knowing what can last
Provides a chance to be bold.
For it's time to leave the fold.

This is my life
That trains for the next life.
This is my life
Where I am now found.
Let it continue, this gift so sound.

BKH 2006

Surviving This Loss

You are gone and I am left with this loss.
I always felt that I'd be the one to go first.
Why now? Why when things were so good?

You always said to me, "We will survive."
Yet, what will I do now when it's only me?
As I pick up the pieces and must move on,
What will I do without you my only love?

Surviving this loss with a heart still aching
Reminds me that this void is very vast.
Sadly, I left you last near our quiet cove
Where you now nourish our favorite tree.

I listen to the water lapping the creek bank.
It does lessen my longing, at least today.
I let you go in order to survive this loss.
Good-bye dear friend and lover of mine.

We will be together again, this I know.
Surviving this loss I know I must do,
For however long, until our reunion.

BKH 2010

I Went To The Well

For peace of mind, I went to the well
And came away wanting.
The ache in my lonely heart
Caused a moment of despair.

A memory seen in the reflecting pool
Creates in me, still, a bit of hope.
What if what I went looking for
Was this shadow following me?

I see the sun and sense its purpose
But came away wanting more.
In my mind I can still hear me
Asking for inner peace thought rare.

When speaking of one's release,
How can it seem so utterly simple?
Still, the time comes for each of us.
Our very own day of reckoning.

A journey joined in true spirit
Requires total commitment.
I do feel completely blessed
At the end of my Earthly reward.

For peace of mind, I went to the well
And came away wanting.
But the ache is now gone
From my heart and soul.

This growth I have rightly gained
Is the deserved fruits of my labor.
I lay me down once and for all,
Only to get up on the other side.

Now I rise and do fully realize
Death was a door and nothing more.
I am awake and free to fly where
My spirit would dare to go.

Fully, I rejoice for this reason.
It was my freedom of choice.
For peace of mind, I went to the well
And found it was within me.

BKH 1979

The Voice That Asked To Be Heard

I heard, "Do you want to listen?" I said, "I think it's time!"
The Voice then said, "On the ladder of life you are between
"The fifth and sixth rung." "How many do I have to climb?"
I asked. And the Voice said, "You don't, but by your own
"Choice your climbing shall go on forever." The Voice
Continued, "In days past you have proven your ability,
"In the face of adversity on both personal and public problems,
"To make the hard decisions. You have seen failure and you
"Have seen success. One admonition offered heart to heart and
"Spirit to spirit is this: If you truly reflect you will see that you
"Have at times given up on yourself by doubting your capacity
"To carry you to the completion of some projects in your young
"Life. Do you agree?" I said, "Yes, that is a fact of life I am facing."
The Voice then said, "That is a step in the right direction and
"Your goal should be to resolve/pursue success until achieved."

It seemed like the conversation went on for hours. I didn't
Remember everything said, but did recall hearing, "If you remember
"Nothing else from this conversation let it be this: YOU ARE YOUR
"OWN PROBLEM, *AS YOU ARE YOUR OWN ANSWER!* What you
"Do determines where you are on life's ladder. Lastly, as you climb,
"Keep a hand out to help those below you and there will be, from the
"Rungs above, a hand out to help you." I remember saying,
"The wealth of your words shall truly help me. Thank you.
"One day we must talk again..."

BKH 1980

Found In The Forest

Walking through the forest alone,
Though really not alone,
I breathed deeply and said,
"It's good to be alive!"
Was it the trees that softly
Whispered to me, "Yes, yes it is!"
Or was it a spirit beyond
Who felt my presence and knew
I would appreciate a response?

With the forest floor as a cushion,
I quietly walked on, further and further
Into the forest, knowing there would be
A clear path before me.
When I was able to see ahead,
I saw a bubbling brook
With a beautiful bridge that graced its banks.
As I drew closer, I saw myself on the other side.
I looked at myself and myself looked at me.
We instantly knew why we were there...

In a scene so serene, we walked toward each other
And met in the middle of the bridge.
With our embrace, we merged in spirit
And became one in heart and soul.
A single cloud shared happy tears
And a light mist fell silently.
Through the sun's rays came a beautiful rainbow,
Which formed a glorious canopy.
I sensed that such a union,
At a moment like this,
Was a rare privilege.
I had found myself in the forest.

BKH 1984

The Pawn

One day not too long ago,
On the chessboard of life,
I heard the pawn before me say,
"Where are you bound?
"What do you hope to achieve?"

I heard myself respond,
"Each move I choose to make
"Must be toward the 'end game.'
"Life's strategies require adapting.
"I shall always do my part.
"I want to grow, I want to sow seeds
"That reach for the light beyond.
"I hope to put pride in its place
"And always acknowledge my Maker.
"I desire to move onward and upward."

The pawn smiled and softly said,
"Are you a dreamer or a doer?
"Will you be patient if necessary?"
I paused and then replied,
"I dream and desire to do more
"But realize I must be patient.
"Each day as I stride and struggle
"I will look to the end to learn...
I listen for words of encouragement.
"They come to me more and more.
"Today my future is mine by taking action.
"Tomorrow is but a step I must take.
"I shall go forward and feel blessed."

I moved off and around the pawn.
His words were now only
Whispers waiting for new ears.

BKH 1984

Our Inner Music

As we listen to our inner music,
Invisible yet powerful magnetism
Has quietly drawn us together.
We see through the windows of our souls.
Wonderful are the feelings when we are as one.
An angel anointed us with tender touch
And acknowledged the power of our love.
Holding each other in our heart of hearts
Honors a promise kept until this life we part.
Comforted by faith and love, our inner music
Does soothe each other's soul now and beyond.

BKH 1984

Lost Moments

Many, many times
During my temporary life,
There were moments which
Required immediate decisions.
In looking back at past crossroads,
I know there have been lost moments.
If there is pain in a backward glance,
The lesson for the future should be
For me to absolutely realize and
Act upon my truest intentions.
Accept this moment in time
And make the most of it.

BKH 1984

At A Crossroad Looking Beyond

Again, comes another major crossroad.
There, with a bold decision before me,
I stand having great confidence in myself.
What comes next may not be clear,
Still, I have grown since the time when
Last I stood at a major crossroad.

Old soul of mine, we have come
A long way in such a short time...
This brief reflection puts the past
In perspective and serves as the
Stimulus to step forward and strive
Toward an expanded field of service.

With an inner calm that quiets all fears,
And though the path isn't completely clear,
I know the unknown can be conquered.
Mine is a noble hand that holds the
Lifeline which will carry me along by
Applying right thinking at any crossroad.

BKH 1984

The Child In Thee

Comes now the child in thee.
Boldly bursting forth at birth
With a deserving desire to be free.
Grow strong while on this Earth.

Bright eyed and with energy so full,
Teach those around you to feel
Our Maker's positive pull.
And always strive to help and heal.

Let the magic of your music touch
Tenderly all who come your way.
As you know, it doesn't take much
To brighten someone's day.

Do continue your zest for living.
Be strong, be bold and keep hold
Of the feeling gained by giving.
And cherish the Maker of thy mold.

Growing up isn't growing old child
When you take faith as your friend.
So don't be meek and don't be mild,
 Because today is not the end.

When you seek the Center of it all,
And go forth with a brave heart,
Always stand fast and do stand tall
Knowing the child in thee is smart.

The world beyond what we can see
Will surely need noble spirits like you.
So, journey on for you and me
By keeping thy child always in view.

BKH 1984

Keep Sight Of Your Dreams

Believe that you can climb any mountain.
Do not limit your imagination.
Live with an attitude of gratitude.
Cherish memories but keep sight of your dreams.

Be true to yourself and your loved ones.
Clarify your convictions and commit.
Act, but never react in anger.
Keep sight of your dreams through your deeds!

Always keep hope alive.
Have the courage to face yourself.
Put any hint of procrastination in its place.
Keep sight of your dreams through right action!

Be one with family and yourself.
Nobility of spirit never needs an explanation.
Risk taking is required for the reward.
Keep sight of your dreams by giving it your all.

If the only way out is through, then drive on.
Have your zest for life balanced in purpose.
Seek the Center as the bountiful Source.
Keep sight of your dreams through the power of spirit.

Forever hold in your heart the wonder within you.
Feel triumphant for holding to honored values and vows.
Live life well and finish with a flourish.
Keep sight of your dreams through commitment.

Let perseverance propel you to greater growth.
Right action is not having to look over your shoulder.
Rewards are gained through the journey.
Keep sight of your dreams and bravely go forward!

BKH 1984

Oh Harmony

Oh harmony,
  You child of the ages,
  Let us look at past pages.
Oh harmony,
  Humanity has let you down,
  And you have a right to frown.
Oh harmony,
  Mankind has hurt you child,
  And too often has run wild.
Oh harmony,
  Improving the stature of sages
  Can help children of all ages.
Oh harmony,
  For the sake of our sanity,
  Inspire us for the survival of humanity.
Oh harmony,
  Imperfect is all of the past.
  We pray in the future it can't last.
Oh harmony,
  Connect with children of all ages.
  We can do it, if even in stages.
Oh harmony,
  Though millennia come and go,
  It is about how much we grow.
Oh harmony,
  Show us that humans can make the turn;
  I know it's never too late to learn.

BKH 1989

One Mere Mortal

Oh you Gods with your games.
You look down from on high
And think we mortals are putty.

I know you laugh and believe
Mere mortals can be molded
And twisted into all you desire.

However, it is time you remember,
"Life is not a game; evil is not necessary!"
I hear your laughter, but wait.

Though some have sold their souls,
Not all of us have sold out.
Your games of chance will end.

You have chosen to create problems
That cause much pain and suffering,
And it has gone on for far too long.

Today you will hear this mere mortal,
Or you will speed faster and faster
Toward a hell of your own making.

We do not agree with your choices.
The trail of tears you have caused
Is absolute abuse of the human family.

If you cannot be part of the solution,
Which will solve human problems,
 Stand aside for those who will.

Mere mortals, if left alone,
Are capable of achieving harmony,
If they truly want to embrace it.

As one mere mortal, I choose
To look, listen, and learn
About the value of all life.

I will speak to others who will listen,
And they will speak to others too.
Then we will see you tremble.

BKH 1989

Five Decades Have Come And Gone

Swiftly, ever so swiftly moving through life,
I have been presented many challenges.
Decisions sometimes faulty were faced,
Even when pain had its vain way with me.

Five decades have come and gone today,
And yet my lust for living does live on.
From infant, to child, to boy, even to a man,
I am convinced that I have a lot of living left to do.

Now baby steps have been boldly replaced
With strides that display great confidence.
My belief system grows amazingly stronger
Because of absolute faith in my Creator.

It is with courage, it is with caring, it is with
Character that my life now counts the most.
Yesterday does creep in ever so often,
But it will not derail my calling to carry on.

While once I took short cuts to get by,
Now I pay the price for the long-term gain.
To live is to give and to yearn is to learn
About how to always make a difference.

With my head up and looking to the future,
I let go of the past and do not fear the unknown.
Yes, five decades have come and gone today,
Yet confidently I say, "Bring on the next five!"

BKH 1996

The River Of Truth

How powerful runs the river of truth.
Flowing, ever flowing onward
To where its breadth cannot be stopped.

Many have tried to dam the river of truth.
Momentary success succumbs to defeat.
Coins dropped in any wishing well
Cannot change the end result.

The river of truth
Speaks to the heart of humankind,
"As life is about growing, live and let live.
"Through good thoughts and deeds I am purified."

Now, in whatever worlds we find ourselves,
We are given a sacred duty
To protect and defend the river of truth,
So that its waters may remain pure for us.

With open hearts,
Let people be available to
The ultimate river, the river of truth.
For it is always available to them!

Never compromise your spirit.
And dare not dam the river of truth.
Rather, be totally open and
Let it flow freely on, and on.

BKH 1997

Resilience When Riding The Rails

While bound for glory that is unheralded,
With whistle blowing and train a rumbling,
As the engineer, you look to see your way.

Driven by a destination called desire,
While the train and tracks are one,
Purpose is delivered by going forward.

The seeker who chooses to remain serious,
When close focus shows life whizzing by,
Knows that wealth comes in many forms.

Today's turmoil, when gone in time,
Surely means that the tracks of life are
Polishing the ultimate bridge, you!

Whenever a way is found blocked,
Do search for the track which will detour,
So that you arrive at your moments in time.

Lest anyone forget, now or whenever,
We'll not miss ourselves when we are gone.
So, make the most of your here and now.

As you travel, guard the spirit you are crafting.
While the rails of life can surely be ridden,
Be aware and choose wisely. All aboard!!!

BKH 1998

Our Greatest Gift

You might ask, what is our greatest gift?
Many will offer up different answers.
For me, I believe it is our enduring spirit.
Spirit that is bonded always to our Maker.

With it we joined this journey called life.
Our book of life is open and we are writing.
What we make of it rests solely in our hands.
Let us be grateful for such a grand freedom.

Cherish the seat of our soul while earthbound.
Comforted by caring power, let us go forward,
Ever striving, today, tomorrow and always.
Take not for granted what is our greatest gift.

Be mindful that pain and pleasure bring growth.
Let purposeful abundance be the fruits of our labor.
So, journey on child of God and be ever thankful.
In time our greatest gift will go to the great beyond.

BKH 1999

A Conversation With God

God asked, "Do you think, or think you do?"
Said I, "'I think, therefore I am.'"
I asked, "Where did I come from?"
God said, "You are of my spirit."

God asked, "Where will your travels take you?"
Said I, "Onward and upward, forever."
I asked, "Whom do I have to turn out like?"
God said, "You don't have to turn out like anyone other than
yourself."

God asked, "What is it you take with you from this life?"
Said I, "Whether bad or good, the karma of my deeds."
I asked, "Have you forsaken me because of past failings?"
God said, "Never!"

God asked, "Do you think little ole Earth is all there is?"
Said I, "You are much, much bigger than this."
I asked, "Who's promoting pain and suffering here?"
God said, "Angels and humans with selfish agendas."

God asked, "Who should be your savior?"
Said I, "None other than myself."
I asked, "Don't misdeeds have to be worked off?"
God said, "Exactly! And if not in this life then in the next."

God asked, "Would you give up your soul for unlimited wealth?"
Said I, "Not now. Not ever!"
I asked, "What will tomorrow bring?"
God said, "Stay the course, do your part and we shall see."

BKH 1999

A View Of This World

Moral is the majestic mountain
That does stand its ground.
Grand is the gift of the rains
That help us to live here.
Healed are human hearts
That give freely in this life.
Love, without any limitation,
Will surely bolster one's soul.

Serious should a seeker be
Throughout this life's journey.
Joining the human family does
Require individual responsibility.
Reward comes through endurance
Of genuine and fortified virtues.
Voices on the wind are aware
Of the changes that are coming.

Costly will the consequences be
For ignoring warning signals.
Wars that inflict massive pain
Cause Mother Earth to cry out.
Failure, even by most of humankind,
Won't change that light makes might.
Constructive effort, by willing spirits,
Can provide a chance for this world.

BKH 1999

If It Were Up To Me

If it were up to me,
Children would never be subjected to prejudice.
If it were up to me,
The planet would stand still,
...if it were up to me,
Until man's inhumanity to man did cease.

If it were up to me,
Seeds of change would be cultivated in fertile soil.
If it were up to me,
No one could coast through this life.
If it were up to me,
People shall produce more than they consume.

If it were up to me,
No one exits Earth before working off his or her karma.
If it were just up to me...
Ah, but you see, it's not up to me.
It has to be up to you and me.
...But if it were only up to me...

BKH 2001

Oh For The Child's Lullaby

Dream not of what once was when
Even the new day shines so bright.
While destiny is delayed by fear,
Action taken makes it tremble so.

Oh for the child's soothing lullaby.
It is the song that comforts so.
Give me the strength by day's end
For tomorrow I'll be a new me.

This education, my life thus lived,
Sets me on the path to my next end.
Eyes open and seeking the horizon,
I am reminded of this time to go.

Oh for this child's soothing lullaby.
It is a song that does comfort me so.
I see the light and can be on my way.
Thank you all for many happy days.

BKH 2001

Who Knew

The drifter lamented a moment missed
Once when he was young so long ago.
Who knew the impact of such a lost love
Until by-gone moments turned to years?
At sea in search of the drifter's soul
Brought him face to face with one fear.
Who knew the pain from his distant past
Could weigh so heavily even to this day?
Ah, what might have been lurks somehow,
Even when the past is but one's history.
Who knew a storm still churned within
And cried out for release and understanding.

A finger pointer plays the blame game
While failing to realize a simple reward.
Who knew a wheelbarrow of internal garbage
Could be dumped simply by letting go today?
Regret jumped up and bit me you may say.
Yes, perhaps that is precisely what happened.
Who knew the most important place to live
Is in the moment, yet working for a better future?
Who knew failure is in the recipe for success.
If "to think is to create," why wait?
Action backed by passion is so powerful.
Now I know, and it's onward and upward I go.

BKH 2002

So Much More

Never believe that so much more,
Between now and whenever,
Is to be viewed as a chore.
Each precious moment is real,
While experiencing this life
With treasures no one can steal.

One good thought leads to more.
And when done daily can
Warm all to their core.
Be not tamed by any terror
That may come your way,
But always admit any error.

What's in store after we die
Is pondered by far too many but
Will be answered by and by.
My heart is lightened today
Because of good deeds done
And braving come what may.

Knowing I and thou can do more,
Let's resolve to do all that we can
As we purify our growing inner core.
By choice, we must not ever quit
This life journey for however long
When striving for the next summit.

BKH 2002

I Have Met Regret

Back when once we met,
In a state of such deep regret,
You came quietly and were open,
As I came with my writing pen.

We both seemed so very sad
Because of feelings we had.
Love wanting to avoid future loss
Won't accept a mere coin toss.

If we each were misunderstood,
Still there really was some good.
Broken promises from the past
Can be overcome by a new cast.

Alive not by any magic potions,
We are through genuine emotions.
Gratefully, to be amongst those living
Requires that we keep on giving.

I have met regret which pains me,
Even as I desire to be set free.
Rising now above all our sorrow
Can be done today and tomorrow.

Yes, time brings us many a test.
Yet we have but to do our best.
Hand in hand we take great heart
Beginning now with this new start.

BKH 2003

It Seems To Me

A cow can't jump over the moon,
It seems to me.
The moon can't leave the earth's orbit,
It seems to me.
The earth appears stuck in space,
 It seems to me.
Outer space is not where a bullfrog can sing,
It seems to me.
There is no drama about the sun coming up,
It seems to me.
Coming from the rainbow ain't no pot of gold,
It seems to me.
On a rainbow, up is up and down is up,
It seems to me.
It's down to the devil if you do darkness,
It seems to me.
Darkness is generally when history is repeated,
It seems to me.
Even now, history has no mystery,
It seems to me.
Mystery is removed by earthly acceptance,
It seems to me.
Acceptance between the seen and the unseen,
It seems to me, brings relief and greater belief.
But then, put simply,
It seems to me.

BKH 2003

Such A Shame

One could say that we are planted here.
So swiftly, as we travel within life's grasp,
We slip through the hourglass of time.

It is such a drain, such a shame, if,
Through connection and reflection,
We do not view ourselves as valued.
Were we not here we could not be.
"I think, therefore I am" is so powerful.

The elusive creature known as the future
Does declare, if nothing can be undone,
Live life fully and with great passion!
Ours is to initiate influence in the world.
And this is a call to perpetual right action.

It is by individual will that we find our way.
Any heart temporarily broken must live on
In order to avoid being but a mere token.
Success is achieved with a sound mind-set,
And truly, a better future is ours to make!

It is such a drain, such a shame, if
We do not make a life contribution.
Intuitively, we really do know this.

BKH 2007

What Might Have Been

Yonder stands Mr. Bull with horns on high.
Seemingly forlorn, he gazes across the lane.
Mr. Bull wonders what might have been?

Were it not for the fence that holds him back,
As the cows mooing caused greater agitation,
His bullness would no longer be a secret.

So, there he stands, stamping, snorting
And pushing on the fence but to no avail.
Still, he wonders what might have been?

His bullness denied by barbwire, leaves him
Aching for cow passion and magic amongst the mooing.
With increased panting, his imagination runs wild.

Oh, to be a bullfrog, if only for a mere moment.
He'd hop the fence in order to quell his craving.
No longer would he wonder what might have been?

In bovine bliss, Mr. Bull would be famous in that field.
The grins on cow faces would make it totally clear,
A bull is a bull and only Mr. Bull fills their bill.

BKH 2007

Choice Granted

What is this fearless free will
That some abuse and use to kill?
While others choose to fill
Their hearts with love, even still?

Choice granted so long ago,
As the tide of life does ebb and flow,
Requires we reap what we sow;
That is, our karma we take in tow.

What is this light among us
That some would dare to cuss?
Yet others choose to make a fuss,
Even as many fail to catch the bus.

Choice granted is a two-forked prong,
Even as one wonders for how long,
What went right and what went wrong
During the course of your life's song?

A gift, to live within the grandest sight,
Does require we carry the fight
And know, not think we might,
It's about doing what is right.

Choice granted remains everyone's test.
And, as we battle each and every pest,
All shall surely be stuck, lest
They know it's in the light where we rest.

BKH 2010

Going Down Memory Lane

When you get on down the way a piece,
Along the road of life, don't be famous for futility.
I know, I know, but don't go chasing windmills.
And don't' be led astray by the pied piper.
Please don't go down Coddle Canyon,
Or stop at Disjunction Junction.
And don't be gain' down Route 666
Saying, "The devil made me do it."
No, no don't turn onto...
Dang, where are you going?
All these detours leading nowhere.

If you're drifting along Discontent Road,
You may want to detour down Memory lane.
Work through your past and get closure.
Once on it, look for the sign that says,
"Your freedom next lifetime ahead."
But before you take the off-ramp to eternity,
Happily, finish your jaunt along Memory lane.
You are required to travel at the speed of life.

Then give a confident wave at the end of the road.
As you get to Lands End, near the top of the world,
Now lift off with great zeal and courageous confidence.
With knowledge and experience you enter the vast beyond.
Those goodbyes said all along Memory Lane shall
Allow for a warm hello at the Healing Center of Heaven.
And know, you will be a survivor there and beyond.

BKH 2001

Dear Mom And Dad

Once when I was but a thought in your minds,
You conceived me as a wanted child.
I am that child, not meek and not mild.

Having come to know myself and my state of mind,
There is total acceptance in my heart of hearts
For my course that has had new starts.

While it began in your womb dear Mom,
Where the first nurturing took hold in me,
It was once born that I was set free.

Those early childhood years passed in a flash.
Yet, to a large extent I have grown with no fears,
And feel blessed because your tears are now cheers.

While there were times that I caused undo stress,
Those frailties and flaws which I must allude
Have taught me to have sincere gratitude.

My youthful self becomes a light in bloom,
Forever in search of the greater good.
I'm grateful as I knew you understood.

From your child's heart, thank you for my life.
You have contributed to my reward.
Now, with my young spirit, I shall turn toward.

Because I am, absolutely, who I am,
I make no excuses and have few regrets even today,
As I stay the course, come what may.

While lessons learned have been sometimes harsh,
They are what have led to the growth of my spirit.
And, Mom and Dad, I just wanted you to hear it.

When my earthly distance run comes to a close
My hope is that I leave a lasting legacy for all time
And venture on in pursuit of taller mountains to climb.

The greatest journey is now happily joined.
So, there is no reason to be sad.
I love you Mom; I love you Dad.

BKH 2003

Here Is How

To make your mark,
Or move rather than park,
Here is how I say,
Take action come what may.

To light the dark,
Or brighten what is stark,
Here is how I say,
Think and act righteously.

To heal your pain
Or help those thought insane,
Here is how I say,
Commit to do what you can do.

To promote reasonable pride,
Or continue to catch each tide,
Here is how I say,
Live, love and do what's genuine.

To have courage as a part of caring,
Or continually invest in sharing,
Here is how I say,
Make a difference wherever you can.

To relish one's ability to learn,
Or transition when your turn,
Here is how I say,
Open your eyes and embrace it.

BKH 2003

On behalf of his Class, the following poem was written and read by Brion Hanks at his fifty-year 2015 Class Reunion for Bellingham (WA.) High School graduates on August 29th.

1965 - Plus Fifty Short Years

Gone where is the symbol of the Red Raiders?
   Taken by the politically correct, such haters.
We experience memories of fifty bygone years
   Where there was both laughter and some tears.
Now our children have children who look like us
   And over whom we rightly make such a great fuss.
But every ten years the carefree kid in us comes out
   Particularly at each reunion we so proudly tout.
Oh, we may have pondered some what might have beens,
   Yet grateful are we for our dearest of dearest friends.
In reality the years slip away and our classmates too,
   But from life let each of us exact our just due.
So smile, take one step and then boldly take two
   For I will always wish the best for each of you.

Brion K. Hanks
Brion.Hanks@gmail.com
www.BrionKHanks-Poetry.com

Postscript: The speed of life is so swift that we may be aghast at how fast the days, weeks, months and years slip away through our life's journey. I propose that we keep our heads up and move forward as we can to make a difference within our sphere of influence. Know that words have power and random acts of kindness nurture our souls...With that, it's onward and upward we go. Safe travels everyone!!

BKH 2015

Love Is Always Better Than Hate

Love is always better than hate.
And please know, it's never too late
To bestow our love in a positive state.

Let the music you choose to play
Soothe you each and every day
With passion as your drumbeat today.

Love is always better than hate.
And to believe it fully on this date,
With heart and soul always in a positive state,
Permits you to firmly say to hate, "Checkmate!"
        If only!!

BKH 2019

What Matters Most

Many seasons have come and gone; still life goes on.
That desire which burned brightly wanes very little.
Oh, to have once said what was sadly left unsaid.

I wonder, what might have been vs. what matters most?
If only, how might individual lives have been different?
Sad on one hand, a heart less full, but it is what it is.

We live, suffer losses and yet daily must go forward.
To speak of past pain could overwhelm a lesser soul.
It can be asked, are we cursed if we live with regret?

Pray tell, what is left after such sorrow or heartache?
Still, let us love those who matter most in this life.
Worthy is our loyalty to the good stars that live on.

We must do what gives our lives the most meaning.
Trust is gained by having the best interest of people.
Greatness is gained based upon life contributions.

We might say, regarding our history, leave it in the past.
Yet music made in life moments still means something.
Of course, we can't unwring bells even if we wanted to.

What is missed most may surprise even the best of us.
And yet we take action with passion that has purpose.
Know that resolve, in the face of adversity, can win.

Do we bravely engage life with love attached to our labor?
The sharing we do garners good karma and is so powerful,
As our best thoughts come to light for making a difference.

Hopefully we are versions of marvels perhaps too long forgotten.
For betterment of the human family, did we give our best effort?
We should agree, what matters most is an epic life well lived!

BKH 2019

105

Turn The Page

If a friend stands on the edge of an abyss,
Speak up and say, "Step back and turn the page."
Tragedies may visit each and every one of us,
Yet life does go on when we turn the page.
Pause and calmly meditate at any crossroad as
Progress requires that we daringly turn the page.
Having established our life's purpose, we must
Bare down, never quit, and always turn the page.
Demand much more of yourself than of others and
Never compromise your efforts as you turn the page.
The road less traveled once had a real trail blazer.
Let us be one and constantly turn the page.
Never make decisions through excessive emotion,
And renounce anger before you turn the page.
Expectations, or even great expectations,
Should always compel us to turn the page.
Recognize the power of why in pursuit of goals.
All the while, control your destiny and turn the page.

At any end there must be a new beginning and
While being courageous, we must turn the page.
Today's experiences bolster us as our spirit nurturer.
Confidently enjoy the ride and bravely turn the page.
When we work our way through grief experienced
We need to survive and should turn the page.
To rise above all destructive upheaval
Requires that we resolutely turn the page.
God may not come when we want him to
But she's always on time, now turn the page.
If life is not a game and evil is not necessary then
We must allow hope to help us turn the page.
To positively believe in oneself is healthy.
At all times we are worthy and must turn the page.
Listen to those striving to increase light and love.
Then willingly participate and turn the page.
Dare to mentally create a compelling future,
And have faith it will happen as you turn the page.
Finally, the pages of our lives really do matter.
Believe it and with poise, each day turn the page.

BKH 2019

Find Your Way

Dare not look in life's lonely lost and found.
Rather, look to those living a life so sound.
Don't linger too long pondering past sorrows.
Rather, focus on what comes in all tomorrows.

For you to always evolve and quietly grow
Means that today you will take your heart in tow.
Be fearless as you absolutely find your own way.
And know that you must truly begin today!

The why is because it's about you and your choice.
So boldly sound off by using your finest voice.
Don't be timid during the freedom you will feel
Nor be accepting of any compromised deal.

Past lessons are always for us the living,
Knowing we have learned the art of true giving.
When you choose to confidently find your way
You will experience the wonder of living life today.

Now visualize it and take action for just that.
And get on with it, stat.

BKH 2019

One Day At A Time

Standing on the edge of a treacherous cliff,
I paused to think about what would be next?
Was it a decision regarding life or death?
Briefly pondering why someone would jump,
I confidently turned to embrace life left to live.
The cliff was just me standing at a crossroad.

Recognizing that living one day at a time
Makes it easier to realize short-term goals,
My mission is to always make the most of
Any and all daily struggles I must confront.
Suffering some setbacks won't deter me
Because I learn from trials and tribulations.

Getting over all losses we shall suffer
Can only be done one day at a time.
Me, as the one on the edge of that cliff,
I assure you, would never short-circuit my life.

Surviving pain or anguish we may experience
Will happen because of our enduring spirit.
For all time it needs to be onward and upward.
Now, let us live happily one day at a time.

BKH 2020

A Tiger By The Tail

What of vices that haunt so many people?
All types of addictions are taking a huge toll.
We observe lives ruined in destructive ways.
Its younger people doing it on a massive scale.
Self-inflicted soul damage by addictive personalities,
And delusion for a "fix" that ends in long-term pain.

Vices or addictions are like having a tiger by the tail.
A price is paid physically but mentally as well,
And yet, today, a new life chapter can be started
In pursuit of our physical and spiritual growth.
To never give up or give in to "demons" is good.
Time lost may weigh heavy on us all. TicToc!!

BKH 2020

River Of Stars

Like a river of stars winding through the Milky Way,
Sometimes a chosen trail will change direction.
Even when destiny bound, we can be derailed.
Yet, an extraordinary life requires staying the course.

Confessions of any kind, when cast amongst the stars,
Can release our inner pain or loss and allow for moving on.
Laboring through give and take makes for a life worth living.
The light of day, each night, allows savoring the river of stars.

Even if marooned on a lonely island for however long,
We are never forsaken whether on this planet or not.
Look to the heavens and follow that spirited river of stars,
Because, we know, the speed of life happens so swiftly.

It matters not how hearts meet but how we choose to live.
So, happily, enjoy the ride along the royal river of stars,
And be forever blessed to live a long life of doing good.
Afterall, each noble traveler gets to navigate this life.

Through caring and faith both in family and true friends,
With purpose, let us dare to do what is right for ourselves.
Then let us be deserving and grateful for prayers fulfilled.
Afterall, when giving freely there is absolutely greater gain!

On the ladder of life, whether now or with whatever is next,
What matters most is to progress as we want for our own sake.
With heart and with helping hands, rest assured, we can.
Upon reaching the end of the river of stars, bravely go beyond.

BKH 2020

Build Happy Endings

Did you hear the one about a
Regal reindeer that granted all wishes?
There was just one condition.
Hmmm? Now what could it be?
I heard, "It's the opposite of sadness,
"And you must articulate a concise answer."
"In a world where dreams are imagined,
"Movers are known to make it happen," said I.
"No. That is not concise enough an answer,
"And it has nothing to do with saints or sinners,
"Or broken hearts or even lonesome blues."
"Can it be about the Golden Rule?" I asked.
"No. While an amazing principle, there's more to it.
"With your thoughts, be not stuck in the lost past
"Because, today, that bell cannot be unrung."
I said, "You're not going to ask me about the
'King who asked his wise men to tell him
'Something that was always true, are you?"
Of course, the answer is, 'This too shall pass."

After pondering the question long and hard,
I have determined it is to *Build Happy Endings*.
What of sessions, confessions and life lessons?
Ah, but back to the question that was asked.
Wherever there is a sad or bad ending,
For however long, I will journey on and on.
Clearly, and without a doubt, hear me now.
I won't ask for all my wishes to be granted.
What I can do is daily apply my own effort to
Make a difference and contribute by *Building
Happy Endings* within my sphere of influence.
As well, I'll share it with others and ask that
They do the same in pursuit of happy endings.
The caveat being, an ending is but a new beginning.
By pep talks and long walks used to find my way,
I recognized a need to deliver happy endings.
With courage to carry on, I will always be
Purposeful, knowing I am a work in progress.
You can *Build Happy Endings* too. Please do!

BKH 2020

Lost And Found

I lost my youth and found maturity.
I lost nearly my life by drowning.
I lost wanting to take shortcuts.

I found building me goes on and on.
I found resolution overcomes disillusion.
I found success to be really rewarding.

I lost my first four-legged friend too soon.
I lost early loves on several occasions.
I lost inhibition through learned confidence.

I found deeds are better than sitting on hands.
I found the will to confidently stand tall.
I found that anytime is train time.

I lost the fear of falling while parachuting.
I lost impatience by choosing the alternative.
I lost part of me when two became one.

I found freedom in a hot air balloon ride.
I found ways to create positive changes.
I found me by cultivating authenticity.

I lost friends in an illegal and wasteful war.
I lost pain by the removal of a part of me.
I lost stagnation by taking sound action.

I found real ways to overcome failure.
I found caring power to be righteous.
I found the benefit of doing the right thing.

I lost compromising with the greedy.
I lost stupidity by learning fast.
I lost kindness when fighting evil.

I found what goes around comes around.
I found the courage to listen and learn.
I found I'm a student and a teacher too.

BKH 2020

Not A Path For Fools

Is fate only for lonely fools
Or would you break that rule?
To look beyond a limiting tool
Is a step by getting on a mule.
Then travel even at a snail's pace,
Knowing this life is not a race.

Your journey once joined today
Brings relief, come what may.
Look beyond an uncharted curve,
And be the master that you serve.
Rev up passion you should feel
And with yourself, seal the deal.

When perseverance does prevail
Do believe that you cannot fail.
Your course is yours to choose
Because, in fact, you cannot lose.
It is a fool who accepts only fate
When we can choose any date.

Embrace pleasure along the way
As you deserve it day after day.
With giving we gain so much more.
And in life there's no time to be a bore.
Don't burn any bridges along the way
As you may return some other day.

Even as life can be messy, most,
Hit the strive button rather than coast.
Still, should you somehow get stuck
Always put on your boots for muck.
Let any "mistakes" you might make
Be learning experiences for your sake.

On a path that's not for any fool
Remember, this life is your school.
Any trials along each daily trail
Are overcome by just setting sail.
Your story is only yours to tell.
Live it first and then tell it well.

BKH 2020

Fully Living Life

We move in a human direction
When we look for authentic good,
And desire to be understood.

To reach real conflict resolution,
Replace failure with a new plan
And believe that you truly can.

As there's no miracle in maybe,
Trigger positive action for you
And pursue what is your due.

Come out of the shadows as
Memories made in the shade,
Sadly, and ever so slowly, do fade.

And then continue to write well,
Even atop a mountain dare to look,
While reviewing life's open book.

The reasons to encourage hope,
Beyond conflict or a road we took,
Are the life recipes we can cook.

In your garden grow what nourishes;
As you quietly move beyond today
Feel blessed lest you lose your way.

As we travel down life's rare road,
All the while in pursuit of perfection,
Do take time for honest reflection.

Then make peace with life's process.
And before the day you choose to die,
Embrace those wanting to say goodbye.

BKH 2020

Ghosts

Some ghosts may linger nearby.
Should you hear any sad sigh,
Know that you must say goodbye.
And you need to do more than try.

It is not heartless to let them go.
And for that they need to know.
Be kind but patiently pointed
As it's their time to be anointed.

Freedom to move on to their next life
Doesn't have to be filled with strife.
Ghosts now present, or from the past,
Need know they don't have to go fast.

But go they must and should today
As change requires leaving this fray.
To navigate a new trail at this time
Is their reward and not any crime.

There should never be any worry
Nor fear or need to be in a hurry.
So, never give up and don't give in
To any ghostly past or present sin.

Every end is but a new beginning
And everlasting life is in fact winning.
Ghosts must step on the path too
As growing is for them and for you.

BKH 2020

What A World We Live In

How many people play the blame game
By pointing fingers at other than themselves?
Many have been careless with their character
Instead of building character that is noble.

Racial divide is broadening as insanity builds
To a point where our survival hangs in the balance.
Family thought to be human is being torn apart.
How long does the past affect now or the future?

What an imperfect world we now live in when
We would allow darkness to destroy the day.
A symphony requires symmetry in sound and
Humanity needs to pull together for its own sake.

Man's inhumanity to man, no longer a secret,
Has to be a disappointment in God's eyes.
Only time will tell whether or not we survive
The growing turmoil that is rapidly spreading.

What a world we live in which appears to
Now abandon itself in such a destructive way.
Children of all ages, forsaking parental guidance,
Have thrown right human relations to the wind.

Angels wonder if it's time to say goodbye to
This earthly experiment gone horribly wrong?
Rejecting responsibility and accountability,
A minority dares to drag down the human family.

What a world we live in which is losing its way.
Can peace and prosperity overcome the chaos?
Being alive and merely hopeful won't be enough.
Will prayer and purposeful action right this ship?
    We shall see and God shall oversee.

BKH 2020

What Was And What Is

Over many millennia, man's inhumanity to man,
As much of this world's damming history,
Is cruelty and suffering on a horrific scale.
In the past there was extensive world famine.
Shamefully and tragically, it still exists to this day.
Disgarceful and inhuman wars for so many years
Have robbed peace of its place in our world.
Pathetic politicians padding their pockets
Continue to exhibit corruption on a massive scale.
Many forms of child abuse still take place,
And are criminal whether past or present.

What could or certainly should change this day
To move what is repulsive to what is beautiful?
Lives altered by so much inhumanity
Do deserve to know freedom and love.
Let what has been lost for far too long
Be replaced by love, unity and humaneness,
Where we, as the human family, are finally "family."

Note, there are not two sides to good and
It's good that must never, ever be lost.
Was it tolerance by Divine Providence
That allowed our world history to be
Shamefully stained by so much misery?
So, what could or should now change
From a past that was so often disgraceful
Such that we really learn from the lessons of history?

Memo! It should never be risky to do what is right?
Real passion in pursuit of world peace can
Produce positive change one person at a time.
Let's visualize peace then act in accordance.
Oh, how most have longed for such change.
With an attitude of resolve to live a life of purpose
We then should allow all to live and let live.

BKH 2020

A Child's Cry

Newly born, a child's cry is warmly received.
Wanting our attention, often, a child will cry.
A child's cry must not lead to sleepless nights,
As we realize a child lives only in the moment.

Through many emotions, a child surely will cry.
To recognize the child in us all is to be human.
Support a child's constructive learning process.
Even now, the child in each of us needs to listen.

Note how people pay attention to a child's cry.
Choosing to cry, what does a child daily learn?
To cry is to shed buckets of tears over a lifetime.
Allow a lullaby to always soothe a child's cry.

Beyond a child's cry, where do we go from here?
Never let fear be a reason for a child to cry.
Teach a child about the glory of growing up.
With patience, allow a child's voice to be heard.

BKH 2020

Just When I Thought I Knew It All

A young child asked me, "Who are you?"
I thought, then said, "Why, I am a child too!"
The perplexed child asked, "You're a child?"
 I answered, "Yes, a child of God like you."

Why can't I see the wind?" asked the child.
"I only know that you can hear and feel it," said I.
This Earthly cherub then calmly asked,
"Why do people hurt each other so?"
I said, "Honey, there are so many reasons."
The child said, "They need more than a spanking."
I grinned and could only say, "Yes, they do!"

"Why do some people die so young?"
Sadly, I softly said, "Only God knows."
"Well then, why do people hate each other?"
"Again, there are so many reasons," said I.
The child said, "Give me an answer!"
"Ok. Religious differences and jealousy are two."
 Looking into my eyes, I was asked, "What is love?"
"Love is a strong expression of affection for another."

"Should I be afraid to be alone?" the child asked.
I said, "Never! Now dare to live an awe-inspiring life."
"Enough questions, I want a hug," said the child.
I kneeled down to experience a tender embrace.
In our world, we need far more children like this.
Oh, to have innocence last so much longer.
Daily, we should nurture young growing spirits.

BKH 2020

Did You Ever Wonder Why?

So many animals do howl at the moon.
Did you know moonbeams create magic?
Why is the man in the moon so elusive?
Oh yeah, to provide earth with tidal action.
When the moon is full it's harder to hide.
Who hasn't been over the moon in love?
Did you know lighthouse beacons shine for all,
And this perfect sun of ours will one day die?
Why does a God of love tolerate a god of war,
And so many put up with the misery made by takers?
Did you ever wonder why empathy is so absent
And few are making an effort to better our world?
Questions follow questions as so many whys?

BKH 2020

The Picture Isn't Perfect

If the horrors of war were no more;
If famine was a thing of the past,
How much improved would our world be?

The terror of far too many tyrants and priests,
Those who I have railed against for years,
If I had my way, deserve Instant Karma.
So, should anyone choose to do harm,
They would experience that Instant Karma;
To immediately feel what they did to another.

I will always shine a light on such despots.
Change can come from standing up to be counted.
Dreams, to be fulfilled, do require assertive action.

While there can be so many unending what ifs,
By deeds, effort is rewarded at the speed of life.
You choose; sit on your hands or be active.
If you don't have burning life aspirations,
Where unfettered determination is the driver,
The only thing holding you back is you!

Anyone who hates fate must then choose
To build on a future that learns from the past.
Success arrives by virtue of never giving up.

I wonder, why does misery love company?
Could it be that someone else's suffering
Makes them feel better? How pathetic is that?
With a call to battle, show up or step aside!
Don't bark from the dark but do speak in the light.
We must do better because the picture isn't perfect.

You can't conquer time so dare to make the most of it.
Finally, from the watershed of your deepest feelings,
You must come to realize only you can save yourself.

BKH 2020

The Willow And I Weeped

The Willow tree has weeped for far too long. I'm saddened on the one hand and angry as hell on the other, because the degree of hell on earth is growing so rapidly. To a large extent, the human "family" is closing in on moral bankruptcy. As a whole, this world of ours is rich with plenty to provide for all. And yet, so much wealth is used to produce horrendous weapons of war. We can ask why; we can even wish but what change will take place? Now, what we think, say and do speaks volumes regarding world failures. Still, it's not too late for right human relations.

If I were God for even one day, I would demand world and religious "leaders" present themselves to me at a mandatory Conference at which I would set immediate new world rules. Any world leader who starts a war will be removed to a special hell of their own making, as well as individuals below them if any war is continued. The same would result for "religious leaders" who incite violence and carnage against other religions and people who follow them. As God for even one day I would drill down as far as necessary to accomplish this simple principle:

Righteously, Live and Let Live!!!!!

No one person, no one country will be allowed to take anything from a neighbor without fair compensation, regardless of what it is. All forms of abuse would stop or those guilty would be placed in a hell of their own making. My success would be rapid and this world would turn to wonderful environments of unity, peace and prosperity. Whatever form of heaven you might call it would quickly be achieved in this world and no one could ever deny it. And if my Creator gave me a week or two more it would absolutely be achieved...If I were God for a day? If only!

BKH 2020

Tales Of A Traveler!

Wow! Where do I begin these tales?
A 3-year-old me escaped on my tricycle
And was off to see a train passing by,
But was rescued by a saintly Samaritan.
My parents quickly learned to watch me closer.

A 10-year-old me went to the local lake and
My favorite Uncle saved me from drowning.
PS, I learned to swim three weeks later.
A 16-year-old me was in a car wreck that
Luckily did not, but could have killed me.

A 20-year-old me journeyed far from home and
I had to face the depths of deep, dark despair.
My spirit remained free and helped me to survive.
A 28-year-old me began travelling married life.
The tales of those last 48 years would take a book.

Lots of growing for my striving spirit on that trip.
Choosing to, a 40-year-old me went back to college.
Four years of working nearly full-time was hard.
The 44-year-old me began an elevated work stature.
The 66-year-old me started retirement, well sort of.

The 70-year-old me began to feel aches and pains.
Age caught me and I knew I was not a spring chicken.
There is much more traveling in my mind these days.
My tales of travel shall go on for a long, long time.
I expect it to continue beyond this challenging life.

BKH 2021

What Looms Large?

Overcoming fear to find favor
Can be found in a life fully lived.
Avoiding the straw that can break
The back of your life-long goals
Requires confronting evil where you find it.
Why? Because so many look the other way.

Never get lost in a zoo of those
Who will always pull you down.
A world hanging in the balance
Teeters on the brink of extinction.
What looms large, dear earthling,
Is our planet evermore vanishing.

It's never to late for right action,
Particularly on an individual basis.
Differences shouldn't result in violence
Or the starting of senseless wars.
We all should be guardians of life.
Yes, you and I have responsibility.

Through choice, differences
Can diminish by the day.
To reimagine our world now
Free of war, famine and fear
Is to establish heaven on earth.
Will world citizens make it happen?

BKH 2021

Righting Wrongs

How long should we hold on to anger
Or wonder how we can right any wrong?
How do we move from too many days
Of darkness to wanted increasing light?
While hope is a starting point for us all,
Action is the ultimate solution for success.
If there's a will then know there's a way.
And remember, we always have choice.

Who is that slowly crawling out of hell
And wanting to hinder or haunt us now?
Life is so precious and certainly so swift.
Random wondering won't right any wrong.
Yet, let us never have a date with hate.
Allow trust and love to be change agents
As a means to avoid barricades to love.
And in a perfect world, let us do no harm.

Are we one day bound for a long journey
Through the stars on the back of Pegasus?
First, get on with righting wrongs we can.
Wonder not about what might have been.
Those are bells that we can never unring.
Reconciliation can overcome wasted time
And promises fulfilled will fuel our travels.
Now make it happen through righteous action.

BKH 2021

The Pain Of Betrayal

A young woman sitting under an old maple tree,
With hair so golden gently waving in the breeze,
Had such a sad look which caught my eye.
She had not observed me drawing closer.
"Why such a sad look," I kindly asked.
With no response I asked, "May I sit with you?"
She looked up and whispered, "Sure."
Facing her, but not too close, I said,
"I sense that you are in some type of pain?"
In that moment she could only nod her head.
Looking into her baby blues I said, "How can I help?"
Nearly in tears, "You can't change what happened."
"Ok, but I am a very good listener."
There was a pregnant pause as I waited.
She then said, "A week ago I lost my grandma and
"Today I confirmed that my boyfriend cheated on me,
"And did so in the worst way with someone he didn't love."
"I am so sorry for your loss. Was his cheating
"A violation of a mutual agreement you had together?"
"Yes. We agreed to wait until we were married and now
"My heart aches because he broke our sacred agreement."
"He was a fool who destroyed your trusted love but
"You can expect he will come begging you to forgive him."

"There is a saying, 'burn me once shame on you, burn me
'Twice shame on me.' Now, you have to decide whether
"Or not you can move past the pain he has caused you?"
I continued, "Regarding him, if you wonder about future trust,
"Do not give your answer right away, but do think on it.
"You are now in control of your immediate destiny,
"And rest assured, you have the moral high ground."
She said, "I just don't know what to say or what to do?"
I said, "I get it. Again, take whatever time you need
"In order to come to the decision that you can live with.
"Should you decide that you will not continue in that
"Relationship, know this, the Universe will bring
"Someone else into your life, and you are deserving."
I slowly stood up and she stood up as well.
I said, "Hand shake or a hug?"
She leaned in to exchange a warm hug.
In parting I softly said, "Always remember,
"Tomorrow is a new day and you will find your way."
She smiled and walked off, even as I wondered
What decision would she ultimately choose?
My thoughts turned to a friend's similar story,
And the pain of betrayal reared its ugly head.
Sadly, this wicked pain touches too many.
What we say and what we do does matters.

BKH 2021

Follow The Leader

Warriors are willing to follow a leader and
Always hope that the cause is righteous.
Death does one day come for each of us.
Even when going to war, warriors know it.
Terrible are those times in human history.

Courage has been raised up from past ages
And allows people to brave the unknown.
As well, self-awareness helps us to grow.
To see the light is to know what is right.
Finding our way requires staying on the path.

Does tragedy and triumph fit into one's life?
A truth chaser should never, ever quit, and
We are never too late to kick habits of losing.
Now, is the direction you are headed in
The one that you really want to travel?

While immersed in living, it matters not
Whether you are a follower or a leader.
Even a leader can stall in a lost and found.
We must not fall behind when living life or
Stoop to being a shallow or superficial person.

I wonder, are we simply on loan to this life?
If life arches stand because of keystones,
What is the keystone supporting your life?
We should support it by our daily actions.
Know that seeds we sow do grow and grow.

A call to action requires that each of us
Never allow life to get in the way of living.
Daily, let us make the most of our choices.
Follow a leader, yes, within the realm of
God's freedom bestowed upon each of us.

BKH 2021

Avoiding Sinners

I've been told
That even a heart of gold
Can't save all sinners.
It's not for me to say
If anyone is saved in a day,
But life winners shouldn't run with sinners.
Do you think
That when you choose to drink
You should congregate with sinners?

Are we completely made,
Or hiding in the shade
Of so many reckless sinners?
Wisely choose to turn the page,
Even when looking for a sage,
As part of freedom from foolish sinners.
When we decide to mettle
And are found in a hot kettle
Look around, you will see sinners.

We would be smart
To immediately start
By getting out of a pot full of sinners.
With each new day
We should move further away
From a herd of contagious sinners.
As we always have choice,
Let us find our sensible voice
And value the wisdom of distance from sinners.

BKH 2021

Soulful Redemption

What treasure can we redeem each day?
Or is redemption down the road apiece?
When a life is saved, what happens next?
If viewed on a road that is going nowhere,
Do we accept the expected or hunger for more?
With eyes wide open, and a frame of mind
That desires the unexpected even more,
Remember to always climb out of any pit.
Yet, never contemplate selling your soul.
So, are you who you need to be or not?
Obviously, we have to stay alive to thrive.
The lonely ones seek any looking glass
In hopes of seeing what is still unknown.
Surely it's not to shadow some pied piper?

Most often, any price we have paid in life
Is the result of our wrong action or neglect.
While story tellers woo us with legends,
Listen if we dare but think for ourselves.
Soul redemption requires one's right action.
Should we wander, keep sight of our road
And never, ever linger in any lost and found.
A life sign says, "Choose a long-term purpose."
Soulful redemption is only within our control.
Righting wrongs, building up to brave each day
Allows for individual and sound soul growth.
Embrace life struggles and choose well.
Labor we must, even for soulful redemption.
Now, let us proceed at the speed of life!

BKH 2021

Essay

God for an Interim Period of Time

Written by Brion K Hanks

Begun in 2008 & Last Revised in 2021

God for an Interim Period of Time

Due to the defiant and often evil actions of some high-raised but warped angels, the Earth Experiment I allowed to take place now causes me to say that they failed me; they failed you my human family; and sadly you are failing to a point that I must step in and take control, lest your world be lost.

My disappointment borders on disgust such that immediate intervention is necessary to stop damage being done which is inhuman to a magnitude that affects more than Planet Earth. In a mere few thousand years, with the last one hundred years demonstrating rapid acceleration toward total doom, there has been virtually non-stop warring led largely by religious zealots and unconscionable "conquerors" who justify their shameful conduct by using the various names given to me. No more I say!

Oppressing methods of terror used by all tyrants stops now! My patience is beyond broken with these religious and world leader types who use overt and covert schemes to mislead and grossly abuse my Earthly children via their lip service, lying, outright hypocrisy, genocide, even mass extermination, along with slavery and intentional degradation. These cruel violations by power corrupted, inflated egos and uncivilized self-serving personal agendas that are contrary to right human relations make them guilty of violating my *Universal Law of non-molestation.* No more I say!

Be not deceived, I see and know everything done on Planet Earth. Ripping off my creation has gone on for far too long. Enough is enough! In particular I say to transgressors, but as well to all, *there is no escape from the karma of your own making.* Lest I do not yet have your attention, understand that you are at the ultimate crossroad where choice, not chance, leaves you with but one way to go.

Beginning today, and this is for each and every one of you, there will be instant accountability and responsibility charged to every individual for his or her actions. When I say there is no escape, I mean there is no escape!

My children, this world that was created for you now hangs in the balance. The premature vanishing point for Planet Earth has drawn perilously close. Extreme danger affecting your survival compels me to do the following:

1. By my power, I will force all fighting and wars to cease immediately! It is not necessary that your world be laid to waste. The horrors of war shall be used no more. Thus I say to you, be not deceived by anyone who attempts to pit you against each other...

2. By my power, the obscene wealth wasted on implements of war will be restored to lifting up my children and to repair nature to the point where it can continue to sustain you. For it is a fact that out and out criminal conduct is being supported through the pursuit and purchase of weapons of war while grossly forsaking people who are starving, sick, experiencing deprivation on a massive scale, oppressed to the point of slavery, and for many who are helpless to turn those things around. No more I say!

3. By my power, and tolerating no interference, I will communicate directly to the hearts and minds of all humankind these commands: war no more; persecute no more; deny religious freedom no more; kill in my name no more; treat each other as less than equal no more. And know this; I give individual identity and equal opportunity to everyone, male and female. There is no exception.

4. By my power, every "religious" book which has twisted my truth will be removed from existence. That means those which teach separatism, and exclusion; that use fear to hold my children; that try to justify war being made in my name; that put forward and profess that a specific religion is the only way to me; and those that have grossly contaminated my river of truth...They are wrong!

5. By my power, stop! Listen and unequivocally understand me on the following, there are no ifs, ands or buts. *The only soul you can save is your own!* This bears repeating. The only soul you can save is your own...Progress and personal growth begins with your first step, one positive thought, one good deed, even one day, or one year, perhaps a lifetime...It will take whatever time it takes...But you

will labor as long as necessary to resolve any and all transgressions in order to right those wrongs and raise yourself up. Only you can do it. Only you!

6. By my power, *life is not a game and evil is not necessary.* If you choose to violate today's commands and continue to wreck, to ruin and to keep Planet Earth on a course that is headed toward complete destruction you will be removed to a hell of your own making. Extreme? Absolutely! There is no more mercy for any shade of evil. In a flash, you shall be taken to a knot of hell where you will be held for as long as it takes in order to have you choose to change your ways and see my light. Regardless, you will labor at righting all wrongs you have committed...Even still I give you choice; however, on this one point let me make myself absolutely clear, you are not absolved of anything should you ultimately choose right action and genuinely dedicate your personal labor toward saving yourself, your world and contributing to the positive growth of my universes.

7. By my power, you will work off all karma that is counter productive to right human relations and increasing harmonics. It will take whatever time it takes, based solely upon your personal actions, to right your wrongs. And know this, if you put energy toward resolution, credit is received only when you labor with no resentment, ulterior motive or expectation other than the burning off of your bad karma. This is the way for you to tip my scale of justice to the positive side and begin banking your good karma. It is the only way to regain your freedom. Understand me, you have the choice to languish in hell or choose to change your ways. Consider yourself fortunate to have this choice.

8. The road before you need not be a dead end. Right human relations on a world-wide scale can be the spark to light the way for seeing your world change in such a positive way that it can be nothing short of amazing! It can happen. And yet, if you do not learn peace through understanding, patience through tolerance and that the need to do no harm are my immediate orders today, you stand to see human life on Earth come to a screeching halt. It will happen because of human failure on a massive scale. Believe me when I say. it is only a matter of time.

9. By my power, *it is only through your good deeds and right action that you raise yourself up in spiritual stature and true growth.* Put simply, you get only by giving out what it is you want. Accordingly, there is no reason to fear me if right action is your choice. After all, when using courage, individual character and the power of your spirit you will be instrumental in bringing about dramatic change to a world that desperately needs it. Believe that you can and I will support your righteous action.

10. By my power, when your individual labor is given out through love and you do so unconditionally, meaning with no expectation, your reward shall be the interest gained on your karmic bank account which has the ability to grow at whatever pace you choose for it to grow. In other words, only deeds demonstrate the truth of your actions and to what degree. However, should you languish in self-pity or believe that your freedom can be gained by doing nothing I strongly suggest that you stop deluding yourself because I can assure you of this, you will be stuck for far longer than you can imagine. In addition you had better know this, *there is no pass and there is no pardon.* Rather, there is only the pain and pleasure born of your personal growth. *Without exception, you will work off all bad karma and do so only through your personal labor...*

And by my power, you will take time to rest, to reflect and to become rejuvenated through awe and wonder as you begin to witness lasting peace on Planet Earth. It will happen!

Why will it happen? Because I have directly communicated to all my Earthly children this fundamental law: *Righteously, Live and let live!* My patience is to be tested no more. Therefore the greatest respect you can give me is to live by this simple but righteous rule.

Sadly many have lost sight of what has always been self-evident. The common thread which binds one and all is the eternal part of me, your spirit. My children, close your eyes and think about this. Regardless of the different races found on earth today, you breathe air in the same way. The sun rises and sets equally on all. You take nourishment in the same way. You all have ears to hear with and eyes to see with.

When I listen to you laugh or cry I cannot tell the difference amongst you. The heart within your human body beats because of me...And if you are cut and bleed does not your blood run red?

So, if you fail to lead in a positive manner; if you fail to act human; if you continue to ignore what should have been by now far too many lessons of life, consequences will be swiftly meted out today.

I recognize that frustration, doubt, even delusion may have set in with the majority of my children on Planet Earth. Do you think I don't understand how you feel? Well I do. Do you think that real change won't happen? Well it will. Do you think that your world's condition is hopeless? Perhaps yesterday but not today. Yes appearances can be deceiving. However, I didn't put in motion and place your planet in a special area of my Universe only to see it blown apart by reckless and inhuman acts. There is a grand design much larger than you. Find solace in this. Your human existence is just a stepping stone to so much more.

As I was saying, you have finally driven me to the point where immediate action is required. From this day forward, anyone who attempts to suppress the freedom and individual rights of another human being or to injure them in any way shall immediately reap the exact thing which they inflict on others. Again, life is not a game and evil is not necessary. If you want there to be a tomorrow, it begins today.

Also, you need to know that a sin of omission is not far removed from a sin of commission. Too many people have turned a blind eye or sat on their hands rather than stand up and be counted with regard to stopping any and all violations of human rights. You cannot have an attitude of indifference or believe that you can live by doing nothing. I will no longer tolerate this. Today you know and must never look the other way.

Massive but peaceful action is my call to arms. Arms that labor to build up and not tear down. Imagine the wonderful power of all the world's people working in a concerted way that only builds up; that only strives to see that no one goes hungry; and that becomes convinced tomorrow will be a better day...Imagine!

My children, for far too long you have acted like sheep. Do not be a member of the mindless herd that follows without thinking and which is too often lead astray. You can, you must stand up with an open mind and a heart that holds me near. There is no reason to fear that I will abandon you. With right action on your part I will not!

The fact is you are not powerless. What has been thought impossible is indeed possible. Limitations are only in your mind. History should be just that, history!

Today you are going to break from old conditioning. You will think in a new way. And you will learn that life can be lived in a way that allows for all my children to co-exist. How? Again, simply live and let live only in righteous ways. No greater gift, as your lesson today, can I give you than this. *Righteously Live and let live!* It cannot be more elementary than that. *It begins today.*

Now is your time. Now is your turn to show me that you are truly human and will choose to begin anew. It is your better nature that must truly blossom today! You will now grasp that a good neighbor helps a neighbor in need. A good country helps another country in need. A good world helps to lift up and make whole all earthly children in need. Fair, compensated labor is how all can co-exist. Truly!!

While my focus has been on addressing the damage being done to my world by zealots and religious kingpins in too many countries to count, as well I am addressing people on an individual basis. *Know that I look only to your heart and the true intent of your spiritual being. Your thoughts and individual actions will speak loud and clear to me and there can be no deception.* I will support positive passion but shall take strong exception to out of control action which is used when excessive or blind ambition/emotion causes destruction, pain or suffering...

Obviously I am aware that some people will travel far from me. Yet by my unseen tether they can find their way back. *One of the greatest gifts I have given you is choice.* And I would have you know, I may not come when you want me to but I'm always on time!

Lest you think I am focused only on evil doers, be assured, I see everything that all individuals do, and I would have you know that your good karma is deposited in my Universal Bank. It is there for you to draw upon based solely on your personal investment. Oh, and if my cosmic books reflect that you are bankrupt, believe me, you have but to look in the mirror of life for the person to blame. So, when you labor with love for the greater good, when you labor for light and when you strive to do what is right I would have you know that such individual action demonstrates your intent to improve the principle of right human relations. Draw upon my wellspring to grow and raise yourself up today.

At this moment, let me be clear with the following admonishment. I will no longer tolerate false gods raising themselves up to mislead my human family and who misuse the freedom I have given. You need to know, I am omniscient, omnipotent and omnipresent. I am the First Principle in all things. I am the Center of all and the Circumference of all. And I, alone, am sufficient unto my own creation! For all time my truth is and has been transparent. For all time my truth transcends anything and everything you can imagine. For all time, *I am The I Am*!

Is it possible that hate can be replaced by love? Is it possible that division can be replaced with unity of family, community, country and this world made for you? Is it possible that past failures had to do with the fact that you did not want it bad enough or that fear paralyzed people en masse? Yes it is. Knowing this, today begins with the changes I am initiating? Let me be clear, your survival depends on it!

My children, do not look backward in anger, nor forward with fear, but rather look around you and have absolute faith in me. You shall quickly see that I am serious with regard to all that I have said today.

Be assured, today is a new day! What will you do? However you choose to act, I would have you remember this, test me and suffer the consequences. Hear me and know heaven on Earth. And when you hold a spiritual covenant with me you shall know the greatest freedom.

Is it really that simple? Yes! It's that simple. Now open your eyes. Go forth and if you righteously live and let live, my life stream will reward each and every one of you. All you have to do is keep faith with me only and your world will get better and be more beautiful day by day.

One last point: Tomorrow I am going to speak to you about the wrongs being done to the animal kingdom and to nature-at-large so that you can then work to make those things right. In addition it will afford you the opportunity to be an active participant in saving your world.

And now my children, with the nobility of your spirits, the only thing left to say is *seize the day!* ©

Dear reader, if I can use the inspiration I sensed, along with my own thoughts, to write this essay entitled *"God for an Interim Period of Time"* then it is possible...

I implore you to search your soul and deeply reflect on what you have just read. Then choose to live your life with profound purpose, greater passion and a constant commitment to make a difference in our world. Doing so both in thought and in deed will allow you to take the lead and be a shining example that causes others to follow and want to be a part of positive change taking place. And like a small snowball starting to roll down a hill, your right actions and efforts will swell to mammoth proportions and reach maximum momentum such that they cannot be stopped.

And what did you have to do? Simply commit to *righteously live and let live...*But as well you will be privileged to bear witness to profound and most importantly positive change taking place. Why wouldn't you? Really, why wouldn't you?

We still have choice, at least for now.

Brion K Hanks
Author and Free Lance Writer
www.BrionKHanks-Poetry.com
Brion.Hanks@gmail.com
Brionh502@q.com

I Paused Atop A Mountain

Like life struggles, pursuit of a
Mountain top requires individual effort.
Upon arrival one deserves a pause.
The panoramic view found breathtaking
Stirred mixed emotions which welled up.
The wonder of it fell at the feet of my muse.
As I looked to the horizon, a circling eagle
Reminded me of getting above life issues.
I gestured to the wind with my will
In order to cast out any life doubts.
Pondering a past full of pain and pleasure,
Gave way to some memories that did sting.
Missed opportunities stirred heartache.
And yet, I boldly reached for the moon
As the fading sun set on such a grand day.
Alone with a self-inflicted pause felt good,
As the sight of what's right is rewarding.
It was me and the mountain in sweet bliss.
Encouraged by enlightenment, life goes on.
I gained peace from a pause atop a mountain.

BKH 2021

Living For The Right Reasons

What brings the good qualities out in us?
As best we can, life is learning to understand
By living for the right reasons in all seasons.
As our voice matters; we must always speak out.
The dance we daily do, to round our rough edges,
Starts at infancy and continues until our demise.

As a sin of omission, silence by the masses
Makes people culpable for not speaking out.
Living for the right reasons should be our duty.
Afterall, it is a fact that all lives always matter.
See the light and let everyone do what is right.
 Spiritual growth is living for the right reasons.

Our determined results in each and every season,
By way of our heart of hearts, betters the world.
Know that all deeds are recorded by our Creator.
If I had the ear of the wind, I would whisper
My prayer that's bound for circumference such
That sanity will take hold of all world citizens.

BKH 2021

The Midas Touch

What is it to have the Midas Touch?
Was it some fable or based on truth?
Imagine if all you touched turned to gold;
Would you really want to have such power?
How long could you stand having the touch?
Might you soon want to wash away that wish?

Could the Midas Touch be in thought form only?
And then there's the myth of the Gordian Knot,
And dealing with difficult problems of the day.
Many tried to untie that famous knot and failed.
Even Alexander the Great had to use his sword.
Far too many mortals give up short of solutions.

By choice we can be great at building on a
Better future that is imagined beyond ourself.
This is a Midas Touch which grows one's soul.
So, scatter not our wishes to the wind using hope.
Rather, realize dreams with daily actions driven
By our touch of purpose and righteous motivation.

BKH 2021

Is Forever Long Enough?

Who says forever and wonders if it's long enough?
Perhaps a lonely wanderer is one who fits the bill?
Such an unsettled amount of time leaves us
To surely wonder; yet, let's make the most of it.
If only we could read our life tea leaves today.
What would they reveal for each of us?

Is there such a thing as a life honeymoon?
If only, would life on earth be so much better?
Doubt should be placed in a lock box today
When looking for a portal to the land of those
Living in peace as believers in order to co-exist.
Too many are incapable of living there because
They fail to be one with an interrelated life stream.

Can forever be long enough for the living?
Might it be a rude awakening, in a real world,
To learn that nothing lasts forever in its form?
We don't need drama kings and queens shaking
The tree of life and hoping to change forever
In an attempt to avoid personal responsibility.
For some, forever will never be long enough.

BKH 2021

Turn Up The Heat

A wanderer needs a course correction.
Turn up the heat.
A careless soul is slipping.
Turn up the heat.
A doubtful lover is losing hope.
Turn up the heat.
A treasure hunter's trail went cold.
Turn up the heat.
A person looking for can, can't.
 Turn up the heat.
A child is not listening to a teacher.
Turn up the heat.
A mix-up is apparent about what matters.
Turn up the heat.
A moment to connect was lost.
Turn up the heat.
A chance to make a difference was missed.
Turn up the heat.
Help yourself and help others by
Turning up the heat for corrective action.

BKH 2021

Another Year Has Come And Gone

Freedom found in power of purpose,
And wonderment of a journey joined,
Fills the seeker with steadfast hope.
When imagination is not procrastination,
The seeker atop Mt. Why asks, "Why not?"

And so, another year has come and gone.
What went right and what went wrong?
The seeker wonders and wonders long.
While struggles come and struggles go,
This much the seeker knows, strive on!

With spirit charged and ready to start anew,
Like a rubber band that's boldly stretched,
We let go of the past and are propelled forward.
In pursuit of dreams we shall stay the course,
As success is achieved by who pays the price.

As always, it is best for us to focus on the now.
A frown on a sunburnt snowman means meltdown,
Yet, like the fearless phoenix, what rises is our reward.
Says a grand old sage to every striving student:
"Attempt the impossible and have little competition."

BKH 1998

The Games Gods Play

Oh what games do the gods vainly play
With the putty known as human clay?

This chattel that give thanks to only a few,
Seem used and abused...If they only knew.
Sadly, the winds of war blow worldwide once more.
I wish they'd move on because of planetary bore.
Now turmoil and terror rip mother earth apart.
Even still I pray for a clean new start.
In the twilight of this lonely planet who will pay,
And does judgment come on only one day?

Oh what games do the gods still play
 With the putty known as human clay?

Pursuit of what is searched for even now
Reeks pity for anyone that would willingly cow-taw.
Maker of man, my heart you have firmly in tow
And gratitude from my spirit that can come and go.
It is, me thinks, much, much too late for most
When the unseen presumes to boldly boast.
Damn such angels that dare to play gods
Believing they can toy with us and beat the odds.

Oh what games do the gods sadly play
With the putty known as human clay?

BKH 2003

The Walking Stick

Supported by such a sturdy gift
Gives me the strength to put
One foot in front of the other.
A thought came into my mind.
This walking stick is not a crutch; rather,
It should be thought of as a shoulder to lean on.
Sensing that I was about to receive a message,
Suddenly, I lifted the walking stick to the sky
And actually heard these words,
"Walk while you can and then
Prepare for an even greater freedom."
Upon grounding my walking stick,
It became quiet yet ever supporting.
I walked on in silence but wanted to hear more.
Again, I lifted the walking stick to the sky.
Amazingly, I then clearly heard,
"Treat all things tenderly; continue to care,
"And do understand, to grow is to share."
Grounding the walking stick yet again
Caused me to realize that I only moved forward
While the walking stick touched terra firma.
I traveled on thinking about what I had heard.
Calmly, I wondered what more I might learn?
Yet again, I raised the walking stick to the sky.
The words came like a floodgate being opened.
"Give voice to your feelings and fully express them.
"As a human, you need to be just that, human!
"Because your time on Earth is so, so short,
"You are foolish if you don't make the most of it.
"In other words, you can make excuses or
"Be about growth of your spirit in a positive way.
"Now, ground this walking stick and let's get going."
Faithfully I did precisely that, and I'm on the move.

BKH 2005

The Need

Since action is my major call,
To stand up is to stand tall.
Surely, I only need to feel the pull
For my cup that yearns to be full.

Even still, it is brave angels of light
Hungering for humans to do what's right.
Certainly there is the need this day
For all to embrace the price to pay.

Because a path accepts any feet,
Movement requires taking some heat.
It is with a burning desire to know
That I must do more than just show.

The need does have to be now.
Forget the why; forget the how?
I shall live by the Golden Rule,
And share such a simple tool.

One step taken leads to two,
As I accept what can be my due.
The need should never cast blame
Along this journey for which I came.

The music that nudges my soul
Contributes to making me whole.
This final thought do I now share.
I will always strive to love and care.

BKH 2006

The Winds Of Change

What comes from another birthday passing?
Just another year older, but hopefully wiser.
Thankfully, the winds of change touch me dearly.

What is the purpose of my pleasure, my pain?
Must be to treasure both during a course of learning.
Thankfully, the winds of change touch me dearly.

Why am I, this day, still alive and still aware?
Boldly, it is to give out more of my precious spirit.
Thankfully, the winds of change touch me dearly.

Why should living require any forgiveness?
To help others, but mostly to help myself grow.
Thankfully, the winds of change touch me dearly.

When will the world finally wake up to this fact?
Peace arrives when we righteously *Live and Let Live!*
Thankfully, the winds of change touch me dearly.

When must mankind *accept, on faith, this Universal Law?*
Alas, yesterday would have been too late for me.
Thankfully, the winds of change touch me dearly.

So, where is the world's *will to do the right thing?*
It seems fractured by too many factions spreading fear.
Thankfully, the winds of change touch me dearly.

Where shall I go when once I choose to move on?
Ah, to the unseen where I've earned my station.
Thankfully, the winds of change touch me dearly.

Who is not content and would step forward?
I say, believers in the right use of knowledge.
Thankfully, the winds of change touch me dearly.

Who is it that can come to know the ultimate sanctity?
We, via our hearts, who are connected to our Creator.
Let us pray, the winds of change shall touch all dearly.

BKH 2008

Simple Pleasures Are

To be alive allows us to enjoy simple pleasures,
　When we recognize them to be true treasures.
A breeze caressing my cheeks near a small brook
　Whispered to me as I wrote upon my life's book.

Oh, how simple pleasures soothe my soul today
　As I sincerely fear not what will come my way.
Dreams realized in a world filled with too much pain
　Will allow my tears of joy to mesh with rainbow rain.

I will decide what my simple pleasures are today,
　Or tomorrow, and cherish them come what may.
Simple pleasures can be the life blood we openly see
　To help us through a world where many are not free.

In my garden I am great and never late to stand
　Where I am truly, oh so truly, one with the land.
If simple pleasures are ours through free choice
　Then we must never let anyone silence our voice.

Choose as we will when no one is hurt by such action
　Because the object is to live a life of great traction.
Faithfully drinking from the well that nourishes all
　Does require giving back as we dare to stand tall.

The setting sun and the moon acknowledge me as a star
　When I freely accept that simple pleasures rightly are.
In giving out that which is what we greatly desire
　Will lead me to boldly succeed and never to retire.

Today is a pathway leading to every tomorrow,
　Where living on allows us to overcome any sorrow.
Through effort we strive to work our daring plan
　Knowing that if we don't quit, we can!!

BKH 2019

Light Will Lift Us Up

When we use goodwill to fill our cup
Most assuredly light has to lift us up.
Yesterday's gone and today is a moment.
Yet, never is war something to foment.

By confronting turmoil come what may,
Disputes are ours to overcome each day.
Personal responsibility is a duty for all.
And we must always dare to stand tall.

Who are we to wait until tomorrow
When we can alleviate any sorrow?
Light will lift us up, we need to know,
Based upon the seeds we daily sow.

We ought to be a friend to our self
And never place our dreams on a shelf.
Always be in the mood to boldly love
And smartly seek guidance from above.

Being assigned now to Mother Earth
Means we should cherish our worth.
In search of the esteemed all knowing,
We must be devoted to keep on going.

BKH 2020

Thank You For My Life

Conceived and wanted in this world,
I must say, thank you for my life.
Early struggles were overcome
By nurturing and steady patience.

Often, decisions were posed to me
And I was given the choice to choose.
Experience does grow real maturity
Along the trail we call this present life.

Amid seasons of trials and tribulations
We must live to love and to give freely.
A willingness to listen and to learn is
The way in which we grow our self.

Know thyself; to thine own self be true
Are truisms I have chosen to live by.
You have made a difference with me.
So please know, I thank you for my life.

BKH 2020

Hope Now And Always

The flow of my spirit moves me in the direction of hope.
I choose caring power over selfishness and hate.
Always, as a life helper, I look for like-minded people.
In the face of adversity, optimism can grow triumph.
Empathy and hope will help me to venture on and on.

Circumstances beyond my control will not crush me.
My choices will be reasoned upon when facing adversity.
On the ladder of life, I will reach out to help people up.
Hope now and always means I can achieve my goals.
I will remember, at worst, any end is a new beginning.

To emphasize the positive is to drive hope ever forward.
On a down day I will remember, tomorrow is a new day.
I will dare to dream big and believe they can come true.
My spirit, like a candle's light, knows the power of hope.
And my hopeful action will lead to my personal growth.

BKH 2020

Noble Endeavors

A noble endeavor is not sitting on your hands.
Through the power of choice know what is right.
Be a good listener and never stop learning.
And always be on patrol to defend the truth.

A noble endeavor is to labor only with love.
Don't let anger derail you from your goals.
Release it and be freer than you were before.
And use encouragement to motivate others.

A noble endeavor is to daily eliminate what ifs.
As well, be moved by sincere and shared feelings.
Ours is to live with a heartfelt attitude of gratitude.
To bring us closer to loved ones, show we care.

A noble endeavor is to give out what you want,
And walk the road of your choosing not the plank.
Never allow an attitude of "whatever," to infect you.
Recognize that family and friends matter most.

A noble endeavor is to grow the fire of our spirit.
And our better nature needs to feel good about life.
So, realize that as a giver you become a getter
By helping others to find their happiness too.

A noble endeavor is to hold fast to empathy.
Live best by knowing the truth sets you free.
A rising sun should not set on so much misery.
On that we can surely ask, Why God? Why?

A noble endeavor is embracing the good in all.
The loves that we have lost should live on
Through the good we must do day by day.
And noble endeavors must never be denied.

BKH 2020

The Stepping Stone

Seemingly so big when we were so small,
The stepping stone that we each own
Is ours for moving in a direction we choose.
Such a landing, even one stone at a time,
Indeed, does require we take that step.
No one should want to go backwards.

Ripples on an inviting pond do disclose
That a brave effort was here made known.
Each stepping stone touched gets us
Closer to a given destination we desire.
Stuck on a stepping stone may feel lonely
But it need only be for a mere moment.

Stone by stone, a leap of faith for everyone
Leads to life gains; yet know we are not done.
When the wind is now warmly at our back,
We step up and boldly hold to our own track.
Every stepping stone reached does mean
We are living with purposeful goals achieved.

BKH 2020

Love Will Find A Way

Are you ascending or descending through life?
Did you live it where self-inflicted harm filled
Your heart and made a prisoner of your soul?

The karmic scale of one's life knows the answer.
It may be sad to say if one concludes it's true;
Even still, trust that love will find a way to help.

Was it foggy thinking or missed opportunities?
If you really believe life messes are not fixable
Then how do you cope with today or tomorrow?

Humanity, often sacrificed by intentional cruelty,
Doesn't need pathetic drama kings or queens
Who impede efforts to save this world of ours.

Darkness is unacceptable to worthy humans.
Soul ambrosia, and I mean food of good gods,
Feeds striving spirits that support light and love.

Personally, any stain or pain of loves lost,
It's sad to say, may haunt some even today?
Yet, a survivor is demonstrated by being alive.

With our desire to expand the stream of love
That has been freely gifted to all of humankind,
We must push back so much surging darkness.

Our growth occurs through making life corrections.
We should never complicate the simplicity of things
But should accept, and allow, that love will find a way!

Journeys once joined hunger for unity of purpose.
It's important we come to know peace of mind and
Bravely accept that, indeed, love will find a way.

BKH 2020

Choice Or Chance

Who is it that kowtows to chance?
Assert your will and let it be the drill.
Why succumb to pure happenstance?
Is a deceitful destiny named chance?
Put doubt to rest and deliver for yourself.
It is best to use your voice for choice.

Daily, overcome any fear of failure.
Do not join the procrastinator's club.
Languish not between choice and chance.
If the meek take action then most will.
Be empowered through righteous choice.
Stand proud atop your own mountain.

Labor with love and strength from above.
Recognize gratitude as a worthy trait.
This life is a gift that must not be wasted.
Throw off restraint and relish your freedom.
Know that it's best to believe in yourself.
Sound off and proudly sing your life song.

Overcome any and all bumps in the road.
Dream, then initiate your action of choice.
Have no regrets with the life you must live.
Allow choice to be the victor over chance
By leaving a legacy that sets chance aside.
Then be content with having lived by choice.

BKH 2020

The Mountain And The Man

Yonder stands a mountain so imposing.
It's been percolating for millions of years.
Picturesque and bountiful in many ways,
Yet craggy, weathered and a challenge.
Even hidden or peeking through the clouds,
It's a permanent fixture on an imperfect planet.
The mountain does help the entire life stream,
With snow for water and trees for oxygen.

An alluring stature that one man seeks out
Has the challenge of clambering to its summit.
In rarefied air, the man is tested by the climb.
Only the top will be enough for a striving spirit.
One step at a time, pushing through the pain,
 A seeker rises above self with such a pursuit.
Every day, an oath is only as good as its giver
And verified by steps taken on this life's journey.

The mountain and the man, linked in a moment,
Are joined because we never, ever walk alone.
Sometimes struggling with each painful step,
The man did contemplate quitting this climb.
Yet nurtured by nature he had to continue on.
Alone with is thoughts, climbing step by step,
 Altitude gained was similar to life's struggles.
Nothing is achieved without going through it.

BKH 2020

Turn Takers Into Makers

Look for those who choose to change,
Knowing nothing is gained without labor.
It's best to live life as a selfless maker.

A maker should never shame any taker.
Rather, strive to turn takers into makers.
Practice brings on success through doing.

If you let the sun go down on failure,
Remember, tomorrow is a new day.
Overcome failure with corrective action.

Don't ask a mountain mystic for answers.
Self-meditation can do one wonders; now,
Listen to your inner voice and change by choice.

Makers master their own environment
By cultivating character and reputation.
For your sake, grow purpose in your life.

Takers can learn by allowing makers to
Reveal the joy of making in any moment,
And by congregating with selfless people.

Common effort can be thrilling and worth it.
A maker has strength of courage and caring.
In pursuit of being human, empathy is amazing.

Takers can learn to put a hand out to others.
Their success is to mirror a selfless maker.
It can become so effortless and rewarding.

Daily, time will do what time certainly does.
Waiting for no one, makers are movers
Who never avoid an opportunity to teach.

Takers can learn the merit of being a maker.
Be not some wild and menacing mustang
Trying to heard humanity into submission.

Never let slip away your reasons for living.
Fear is conquered by years of success.
Be a maker helping to grow lifers for love.

BKH 2020

Turtle Talk

"Can't you see that I'm eating water melon here?"
"Well, you did say for me to ask for turtle talk."
"Did I? Hmmm, tell me, why would I do that?"
"I'm told you are the turtle muse talking atop Mt Why."
"So, are you some kind of monster standing over me?"
"Nope. Just some lowly human seeking turtle wisdom."
"Well then, take a seat and I will answer your questions."
"Ok, how the hell did you get on top of this mountain?"
"Too simple of a question. After all, one step at a time."

"Well then, why is our sky the blue color that we see?"
"Scattering of sunlight off the molecules of the atmosphere."
"Really? Alright, how many stars are there in our universe?"
"I am not an astronomer but try 100 sextillion, give or take."
I asked, "Why do you suppose humans can't get along?"
"Easy! Deranged 'angels' who were allowed to populate Earth."
"What!! Was this some kind of experiment gone bad?"
"Seems pretty obvious to me. You humans are pathetic!"
"Why are there so many races and languages on Earth?"
"Easy! 'Angels' brought them from far away worlds."

"I have to know, why has there been a failure to coexist?"
"Easy! Different religions thinking only their way is right.
"Enough questions, I'm headed down for turtle tango.
"When the girls come a calling, I aim to satisfy their urge.
"You get that don't you as 'just some lowly human?'
"Enough questions. Come back after this mating season!"
There I was, still wondering, with so many questions.
How long is mating seasons for turtles? I mean, come on!

BKH 2020

More Than A Diamond In The Rough

All that I have earned is found
Within my heart, mind and soul,
And goes on with me always.

I draw upon the divine energy
To give me strength anew,
For it shall see me through.

Truly alive is my spirit
As I evolve and grow
Toward the next realm.

More than a diamond in the rough
Deserves the grand polish
In order to feel fully worthy.

The search for self may seem
Perhaps painful at times, yet,
The only plan worth pursuing.

I will surrender to the moment
As a means to accept right now,
And affirm my quiet resolve.

Bravely, I will cross each bridge
To grasp the incredible power
That is mine day in and day out.

Now, the degree of polish
On this diamond, my spirit,
Propels me forward and to carry on.

BKH 2001

Live Life On Time

To enjoy fresh air on a grand sunny day.
To wait for and wish upon a shooting star.
To use imagination while reading a book.
To pace and faithfully pursue our maturity.
To hold the hand of the one we love.
To extend a hand for helping another.
To listen intently is showing we care.
To believe in the person we yearn to be.
To be connected to our ever-growing self.

To pick oneself up after any failure.
To willingly accept a hand if needing help.
To cherish the value of our true friends.
To live with passion for life-long learning.
To make a difference wherever we can.
To hold close those who enrich our lives.
To dream big and strive to make it happen.
To get on with living and never give up.
To live life on time today and tomorrow.

BKH 2020

The Lantern

Life doesn't get in your way so live it.
Love it too and get on with your passion.
A lantern can illuminate our way if lost.
Overcoming self-imposed boundaries
Every day is to be your price for life.
Wandering off our chosen path can
Be costly and bring potential heartbreak.
Should the fire in your lantern go out,
Was it purely coincidence or intentional?
If you can determine the why each time,
With effort, a lantern can always be re-lit.

We must do much more than just exist.
A striving spirit will happily carry a lantern.
So, in life we can always find our way.
Giving voice to the choices we make,
Allows us to embrace our life purpose.
Rest and reflect when you feel the need.
But know progress comes one step at a time.
It is worth it to carry our lantern each day.
Prices will be paid all along the way and
That has to be ok as nothing in life is free.
You won't be held back carrying a lantern.

BKH 2021

A New Beginning And Beyond

When letting go of all that we call our past,
Commitment to change builds upon our future.
So, do something new and dare to do it now.
In other words, pick up and want to move on.
Of course, it starts with a strong belief system.
And wherever you go, bring more to the table.
Picking up the pace doesn't make it a race.
Indeed, moving beyond thinking requires action.
 Listen to learn and teach others who will listen.
Scatter to the wind all that has held you back.
Knowing that a dream can become a reality,
Begin anew and then go for what is beyond.
Afterall, the only one holding you back is you!

BKH 2021

The Magic Of Mindfulness

Mindfulness, as one form of freedom and
Which equals self-investment, grows our spirit.
Yet, do not lose sleep over any mindfulness
That gets caught up in memories too distant.
Nor should mindfulness waver because of maybes.
Day in and day out, even moment by moment,
Mindfulness allows us to reveal our commitment
And it helps each of us to trust our gut feelings.
Yet, be not jealous of any master of mindfulness.
Subconsciously, we know what is best for us.
After all, and to a point, our guardian angel is
There to guide and support us if we need it.
Once found, our own voices need real exposure.

The magic of mindfulness is passionate confidence.
Mindfulness should be utilized to validate our purpose.
It can overcome failure through second chances.
We have but to take the time to perfect our own
Method of mindfulness which will work for us.
Whether it's about the past, present or even
The future, mindfulness will truly serve us well.
Like rain washing the air, mindfulness is the engine
That helps us to know and be true to our own spirit.
While it does require patience and perseverance,
In life we can fight villains and champion heroes too.
Our decisions made in this life are best served by
The magic of mindfulness used on a daily basis.
Now be mindful and meditate on this!

BKH 2021

In Pursuit Of A Great Truth

At terminal velocity, I wisely pursued a great truth.
Through the mist came a white horse carrying an
 Illuminated being who smiled at my perplexed look.
I knew not where I was or who was approaching me?
She leaned down to hand me an envelope with these
Three words written in gold leaf, "A Great Challenge."
As quickly as ever the horse and its rider were rapidly
Swallowed up by the haunting mist, to be seen no more.
Wondering, I stood in silence and heard nary a sound.
Setting pride aside, and with no thought or feeling of fear,
I opened the envelope and there was but one sentence.
Out loud I read, "He conquers who conquers himself!"

Hmmm, and of course, the future is ours for the making.
Now, the past can't last; the present is but a moment and
Success comes in many forms even if not satisfying today.
Let's be grateful for what we do have, even as we wonder.
So, know that tomorrow's gift shall be greater success.
We should make the most of today and every tomorrow.
Because rigorous action can generate abundant success,
We can achieve what was imagined when we don't quit.
Believe that it will one day arrive in our reality, and it will.
There's no shame in any failure or if we should fall short.
Our loyalty should be to life such that we give it our all.
Just don't quit the challenge in pursuit of a great truth.

BKH 2021

A Baker's Dozen

1. I am Grateful to have recognized my Creator first and foremost
2. I am Grateful to have the sun, moon, air, water and food for life
3. I am Grateful to have been born into the life I am living
4. I am Grateful to have had confident and caring parents
5. I am Grateful to have received my educational life experiences
6. I am Grateful to have realized the value of imagination
7. I am Grateful to have faced the freedom to forgive myself any failures
8. I am Grateful to have learned from my "mistakes"
9. I am Grateful to have had long-lasting friends
10. I am Grateful to have valued being a free moral agent
11. I am Grateful to have joined a battle of light over darkness
12. I am Grateful to have recognized the power of live and let live
13. I am Grateful to have made a difference in our world

BKH 2021

Footsteps

Viewed as an unending journey, my deliberate footsteps
Are placed daily on a path I choose to boldly blaze.
While any ending surely will have a new beginning,
Our footsteps move us forward to realize dreams.
Today, let us not dwell on what ifs or succumb to
 Being some dismal foot note in the annals of history.

Now, are we wandering through life's lost and found
Or going through that gate known as a living hell?
Might we wonder what role human nature plays in life?
We know that life is living through changing conditions.
I support the keystone of life known as human kindness.
So, let's never be petty people who don't love life.

One day I heard footsteps behind me as I walked.
 Only my shadow was there when I looked back.
And yet there were footprints other than mine
In sync with the footprints my footsteps were making.
The whisper I then heard must be my guardian angel,
"It's best for humans to live life fully and with gratitude."

It occurred to me that a principle found to be universal
Has to eventually take hold in the hearts of life heroes.
We should want for it to be contagious today. If only!
Now, as our footsteps are revealed, we should expect
To be asked, what mark is it that we will leave on
The path that has to become our personal history?

And yet, if we have one foot planted in the past and
The other placed in a preferred future, how do we
Deal with where we are at this moment in time?
If we are to be a real reflection of our best self,
For our own good, let's not get stuck in some lonely past.
Our footsteps should press forward to make a life difference.

BKH 2021

A Happy Heart

With a happy heart
We can choose to
Commence any new start.
With proactive health,
When done for ourself,
It can lead to greater wealth.
Let's live the life we deserve,
Done day by day together,
As the life stream's ours to serve.
While we may get bloody,
Life is for us to fully live
Because we are somebody.

With a happy heart,
We live more fully when
Our compass traces our chart.
Let us never be a burden
Along our life travels as
Soul growth can be certain.
The ways of conveying charm
Are ours to rightly choose,
But let us never do any harm.
So, while here on this earth,
I believe efforts rooted in truth
Do grow our spiritual worth.

BKH 2021

A Growing Me

A fast crawling me led to early walking,
And a life pace moving faster and faster.
Still, I wonder what an ultimate life
Would be for you, and this daring me?
Like a butterfly flittering on the wind,
The weight of worry was washed away.
A growing me overcame lurking fear.
During days of riding the freedom rails,
Early on bound for nowhere in particular,
Each rising sun spurred me forward.

A young me knew being a member of the herd
Would be drudgery, boring and stunting too.
By my choice I freed myself of such stagnation,
And always, I will never settle for mediocrity.
Spirit and individualism that's founded in faith
Deliberately propelled me along my path.
Deeds deposited in my karmic bank account
Pay dividends both in this life and the next.

My journey, looking far beyond this life,
Will daily grow the grateful soul within me.
To be the champion of my own success
Continues to come by way of a growing me.
The endless road remains onward and upward.
By truly living and loving life as a growing me,
I build upon my positive and lasting legacy.
All for a growing me; really, why wouldn't I?

BKH 2021

The Fixer

To find our way in the world,
Through bold leaps and bounds,
We succeed by faith in ourself.

Are the vein really in pain because
They can't see beyond themselves?
Hmmm, who will be their real fixer?

Who are those wanting, even needing,
Some fixer to charm away their ills?
Who could this mysterious fixer be?

Choosers of freedom can become
World ambassadors and will know
They need not look for supposed fixers.

Lives mapped out, or not, are
Made easier when we realize
That within oneself is the real fixer.

Languish not in any lost and found as
Fear can be neutralized and faith installed
When we wake up each day as our own fixer.

BKH 2021

What Changes My Spirit?

Can chilling in the wilderness?
Or being on an island sanctuary?
Or a mere moment of meditation?
Or a song sung desiring lasting love?
Or stretching the tether to my Maker?
The constant; everything changes our spirit!

Can giving out what we want really work?
Or being content with perfection shortfalls?
Or a failure to be even somewhat godlike?
Or could the growing up of the child in me?
Or a decision of getting right with my Maker?
The constant; everything changes our spirit!

BKH 2021

Here Me Now

Here me now, the sun will come up tomorrow.
And there truly is life beyond each and every day.
So, forgo drudgery and do what gives your life meaning.

Here me now, love is a very good remedy for all ills.
Value the treasures found in your heart and soul.
To freely, and always, live to give is rightly awesome.

Here me now, stay the course and persevere with purpose.
You must believe in yourself as you are a gift to our world.
As well, be a bold leader who applies positive inspiration.

Here me now, be your best self in the face of any adversity.
Always remember who you are and be authentic with yourself.
Allow your human heart to be about changing lives for the better.

Here me now, dare to bravely seek the top of the mountain.
Indeed, you have a voice and you always have choice.
So, choose to do the right thing even when no one is looking.

Here me now, never allow anyone to tell you, "You can't."
And isn't it tragic that children are contaminated by hate.
Nobility of spirit grows in strength when we dare to say, "No!"

Here me now, champion success for the less fortunate.
On the ladder of life, it's admirable to extend a helping hand.
Our world needs more people pulling together for its survival.

Here me now, the remarkable river of truth does not lie, ever!
Much of mankind's inhumanness is the source of world evils.
So, be responsible and don't contribute to or condone cruelty.

Here me now, Earth keeps spinning as you are triumphant.
It will be made known; you made a difference in this life.
As in like unto like, let the masses be drawn unto you.

Here me now, to grow we must learn from life lessons.
To blossom we must brightly contribute to spiritual growth.
Finally, a part of our success is to give out what it is we want.

Here me now...after all, it is about time...

BKH 2019

The Karmic Merry-Go-Round

Any barricade to Heaven is self-made.
And for some it's sad as a life does fade.
We all have the ability to set ourselves free
Of the karmic merry-go-round, this life's tree.

Round and round so many do pitifully go
Thinking that it's only some sad show.
Life is real and to steal from self brings pain,
But relief can be realized when once sane.

Seconds of life certainly do tick swiftly away
Even on the karmic merry-go-round, if you stay.
We can be more than caught in a frightful funk
But we should never think our ship has sunk.

Most chained to the karmic merry-go-round
Are liars, cheaters and thieves with no crown.
Languishing in self-pity won't release even you
Without efforts to embrace your authentic due.

It's time to make yourself available to sage advice,
But with your soul's freedom you can't roll the dice.
Indeed, you have a reservation with karmic fire
And need to know there is no one you can hire.

Waste your life no further with opportunities present.
Karmically, you must daily make a verifiable dent.
Openly, place your faith in right corrective action now,
Such that looking forward you can soon say, "Wow!"

You must commence to evolve and solve karma that's bad
And show your worth by burning it off without feeling had.
Know that, without exception, it takes the time it will take.
Believe me now, you must to do it for your own sake.

Confessions seeking absolution will not work as a solution.
Sincere effort means the most by correcting karmic pollution.
Be significant, be authentic and be compelling with your action.
Now use this daily mantra - I must never stop or lose traction.

Any secrets revealed will never seal our personal fate.
Working to get off the merry-go-round means we can't be late.
Be now self-compelled to morally act and agree to never coast,
For it is best to put right all wrongs, as that matters most!

BKH 2020

History Of Being One Human Being

I have made peace with past failures, even past pain, and
Live not by what ifs but through honor and trust for what's right.
I have the courage to listen, the courage to care and the
Courage to build up, rather than tear down, this world of ours.

With any disillusion let us pursue immediate resolution.
Note, the karma we make must be good for our own sake.
Daily, as I go about performing each and every task,
It's been my intention to never hide from the life I need to live.

I chose only to labor with love and purposeful passion
So that my existence never languishes in earthly drudgery.
My ambition and ego are never motivated by anger.
Rather, my focus is the absolute pursuit of the greater good.

A promise to the world - My fate is never rooted in hate.
And I am never late when working through life changes.
For me, mistakes are unexpected learning experiences and
I get that free choice matters most for a life well lived.

Recognizing that a virtuous and truthful life really does matter,
I work to fill my karmic bank account for this world and the next.
It is done with caring power and conviction born of courage.
Freely, I utilize thoughtful ways which help my future self?

Clearly, I know, we will have crossroads during this life which
Should lead to growing and sowing seeds for making a difference.
It's been suggested, confront any demons both in thought or form,
Through standing up against what we view as morally wrong.

The human book of life we write gets added to on a daily basis.
I chose to never join the vast majority of people who
Languish in mediocrity and are stuck in non-productive lives.
Authentic need we be to succeed with a life well-lived.

We should ask, has there been purpose to our earthly existence,
Such that we never, ever, let our wonder wither...? Answer: Yes!
In a world where right must make might, I dared to join in
To influence and contribute my life effort of being one human.

BKH 2020

Pain From The Past

Is this true or is it false?
Can lost love be found
Such that pain is dissolved?
Is there such a sad thing
As the death of some loves?
The hurt of long-ago goodbyes
Causes doubt and what ifs,
And wonder of what's true now?
It is a fact, you have been far
More than a stone's throw away.
Even today, what could I say
Except I'd have met you halfway.

Life lines blurred remain foggy
As love in the past didn't last.
For us, the timeout whistle blew
Such a long, long time ago.
Could we even play ball again?
Wounds fester still to this day.
What or who can heal them?
Even now, in this moment,
Who would make the first move?
In that lonesome realm of regret,
Hope as habit is not helping.
To be able to say "I'm sorry" matters.
Certainly, I am and wonder are you?

BKH 2021

From Rest To Quest

From where the vagabonds stop to rest,
   We can see nature in her full zest.
The trees talk to us and are heard to say,
   "Do give thanks on this special day."

Even still fall colors can be seen
   And send us feelings we find clean.
Yonder runs that great river so grand
   Caressing the cliff on which we stand.

The wind is heard to whisper today,
   "On your journey for freedom do stay.
"Live your lives in touch with reality;
   "Giving all you can to remain free."

We held each other as the sun came out
   And then a rainbow removed all doubt.
Oh Maker of man and the Universe too,
   We do give thanks and only to you.

Do not give up on us we quietly ask
   But protect and commend us to our task.
Now we are off to do our very best
   And it shall be a grand quest.

BKH 1989

Be No Fool Or Tool

Who follows a damned fool?
Who would be a demon's tool?
Perhaps creatures of the dark
Take that lonesome trip for a lark?
One day they must understand
Fools or tools cannot command.
With one's Maker any vows broken
Will require much more than a token.

We are given a great deal of rope.
Let all know there is always hope.
Harder will the road be coming back
But perseverance will find the track.
Should we wander off now and then,
It's good to know we can get back again.
Yes, it's hard to rise above temptation,
But to affirm our Maker leads to salvation.

BKH 1990

The Light Of The Candle Does Care

Each of us can be a noble light
  That day by day grows in might.
We think and therefore we are
  As we journey beyond this star.

Big dreams today, or even tomorrow,
  Can triumph over anyone's sorrow.
If we change from the inside out,
  We will prevail without a doubt!

Identifying choices gives us power.
  Let us never feel we need to cower.
In our workshop we'll work on whatever
  With dynamic imagination as our lever.

We will be bold and dare to think big,
  Knowing a great oak comes from a twig!
There may be many barriers or blocks
  But righteous action is what talks!

Always, the *I AM* and we are spirit.
  Not now nor ever should we fear it.
So smile, take one step and then take two
  As I will always wish the best for you!

On and on you must journey young traveler,
  Knowing here you are but a brief visitor.
As a noble spirit do more than just stare
  Because the light of the candle does care.

BKH 1995

The Train Of Fear

The Engineer on the train of fear
   Pours the coal for many sad souls.
Yet, speeding down the tracks of life
   Simply passes everything in sight.
Who believes they leave things behind
   While riding that dreadful train of fear?
More speed does not help anyone as
   Faster and faster frees no fear.

Those fooled on the train of fear
   Cannot fake the trip they take.
Wailing of the willing and unwilling
   Should send a clear message to all:
What's in your heart and in your mind
   Is with you everywhere you go.
So, why be on the train of fear when
   Faster and faster frees no fear?

Who would envy such sad, sad souls
   That seek escape from themselves?
Surely it isn't you? Not you? Is it?
   By getting off the train of fear you
Arrive at the station known as Freedom.
   The freedom to help, the freedom to heal.
Be admired for finding freedom, knowing
   Faster and faster frees no fear.

BKH 1997

Appointment With Freedom

Freedom comes from knowing who you are.
Why you exist does further that freedom.
Freedom comes from always doing your best.
Having a belief system furthers that freedom.
Freedom comes from living within your means.
Sharing and caring furthers that freedom.

Freedom is giving with no strings attached.
Positive self-esteem furthers that freedom.
Freedom means speaking the truth always.
Courage through caring furthers that freedom.
Freedom is living by deeds and not by words.
Taking right action furthers that freedom.

A freedom appointment requires showing up.
Personal effort changes your life for the better.
Freedom is the gift for taking the high road.
Loyalty leads you to live a life wherein you
Respect the freedom of others and yourself.
Commitment to what you believe in brings freedom.

Being a builder and not a destroyer delivers freedom.
Know that freedom is founded in the Father Everlasting.
Recognition that you are spirit gives you freedom.
Choosing always to covet real clarity of heart,
From thoughts, to words, to action through deeds,
Means you shall be comforted by such freedom.

An appointment with freedom requires honest action.
Your reward is the fruits of righteous risk taking.
Recognition of harmony's inner healer does lead to
A life filled by many appointments with freedom.
Acknowledging that God is Good, God is Great and
God is Giving advances your enduring freedom.

BKH 1998

No Parking In The Way Of Progress

If the lesson for the living were
   No parking in the way of progress,
   Then progress requires being productive.

It has been said about the living dead,
   Many are stalled along the highway of life
   And won't commit to moving forward.

If there is no gain without some pain,
   No parking in the way of progress
   Means change must take place.

Most people would say life is a struggle
   In which a person finds their own way,
   Hoping they made the right choices.

If what matters most to many is only today,
   No parking in the way of progress
   For some, may not matter even tomorrow.

It would seem a shame to will your way
   Through life hoping rather than doing,
   When progress is only an attitude away.

As our world is hurling through space,
   No parking in the way of progress
   Requires that we honor Universal Order.

Herewith, it is determined, stagnation
   Leads nowhere now or ever and so,
   No parking in the way of progress is progress.

BKH 1998

Earthly Watcher

What lens do we look through
When peering out at the world?
Do we see what we need to see?
A watcher we all should be and
It's through watching that we learn.

The power of observation is natural.
Watch for potential and do nurture it.
All levels of emotions can be activated
Based upon what is seen before us.
As well, pay attention to our intuition.

A keen sense of observation will
Pick up on even subtle signals.
We do make many mini-decisions.
It is a fact, we affect people even
When reading them, just by watching.

Radiate out what you desire for others.
Never allow fear to be your motivator.
Don't muddy the simplicity of things.
If we criticize, even by way of watching,
We must have the heart to help.

Go in the direction you are watching.
Believe that life messes are fixable.
If needed, watch to reverse chaos.
As well, be not a lazy earthly watcher.
Yesterday's gone; make the most of today.

Know it takes more than watching each day.
Don't pull the ripcord on this life too early.
Pillars of human growth need to prevail.
As an earthly watcher, a reader of people,
Choose to boldly enrich life with love.

BKH 2020

In This Moment

In this moment,
  The future is now
  And there is no need
  For a time-traveler to ask how.
In this moment,
  I do accept being me
  Because there comes a time
  For all to know we are free.
In this moment,
  I will choose to be selfless,
  And do believe
  I am never helpless.
In this moment,
  Through prayer and reflection,
  I move full steam ahead
  In pursuit of soul perfection.
In this moment,
  It's good to work through any fears
  By way of patience and perseverance,
  As long as there are only happy tears.
In this moment,
  What washed over me is from the past,
  And reposes as my personal history;
  Yet, I pursue a future I will cast.
In this moment,
  It's sensible to minimize any pause,
  Except for a brief moment when
  Choosing to embrace a worthy cause.
In this moment,
  What ifs are wasted on wonder,
  Were I to accept any mundane fate,
  Unless I wisely sound my own thunder.

BKH 2020

Content Or Not

Once when I walked along a swift moving river
I felt unnerved by my need to see around the bend.
Who knew that one who ached to know the unknown
Would be willing to roll the dice for life and then
Be rewarded with what it turned out I needed now?

Acceptance of myself, in such a rare moment,
And sufficiently content to let go of the past,
Allowed me to move forward into a realm of
Living with my choices day in and day out.
Growing in ways that matter have helped.

Moving forward, I'll proceed to the next bend
Even though it may or may not be enough?
For me, real satisfaction is having choice.
In being propelled forward, I have faith that
Ultimately I'll be satisfied with where I find myself.

Anyone who is a forlorn wanderer may
Wonder about the unknown that's lurking.
On the other hand, another part of me became
Content with the present and where I found myself.
Content or not, we cannot escape who we are.

Now counts most; wisdom is making the most of it.

BKH 2021

Always

Sailing, always sailing,
Freely on and fully awake,
Makes me a grateful traveler.

Reassured, always reassured,
I am through experience gained
Moment by precious moment.

Action, always action,
As a part of the big picture,
Allows me to enjoy the ride.

Channel, always channel,
Heartfelt, purposeful passion
Which safeguards righteousness.

Learning, always learning,
As a grand gift from God,
Advances life in the Universe.

Love, always love,
Lifts me up today and
Champions all my tomorrows.

Present, always present,
Where centered on the now,
Helps the student I am today.

Guardians, always guardians,
Teaching me for however long,
Nurture my spiritual growth.

BKH 2021

Do You Get It?

What goes around comes around.
Do you get it?
Earthly seasons will continue to change.
Do you get it?
Don't let your past sabotage your future.
Do you get it?
Believe that love can overcome hate.
Do you get it?
You must be your own savior.
Do you get it?
If thrown into the deep end, choose to swim.
Do you get it?
Make room for love that's always in bloom.
Do you get it?
Know thyself and to thine own self be true.
Do you get it?
Complacency need not be punishment for inaction.
Do you get it?
Mistakes are unexpected learning experiences.
Do you get it?
The truth is a great and transparent weapon.
Do you get it?
It's ok to be satisfied in pursuit of more.
Do you get it?
An ounce of faith is better than none.
Do you get it?
Surviving a loss requires getting on with living.
Do you get it?
If you fall down, the life answer is to get up.
Do you get it?
Today, you still have the rest of your life.
Do you get it?

BKH 2021

The Future

With faith that right does make might,
Bravely dare to fight evil on all fronts.
Always be one to look to the future by
Contributing toward better tomorrows.
Choosing a future that's yet to be done
Is championed by those with conviction.
Accept the call without any limitations and
Let's want it to be bright; let's make it right,
And may it firmly grow by our Creator's light.
For sure, and for each of us, be responsible
With the future we are getting to choose.
It is ours and we should never waste it.
As tomorrow is a new day for everyone,
We must face the future that is before us
And definitely be about making it happen.

Choices confidently voiced by the righteous
Can be realized in ways that are wonderous
When driven forward by one's determination.
Courageous are those who reach out and
Turn toward a future that is deserved.
Don't shy away from effort to get there.
And too, let us take the time to lift up
Others less fortunate than ourselves as
A means to contribute toward their future.
Now, we may ask what is our most important
Purpose today or in each and every tomorrow?
Believe that prayers heard can be answered.
We decide, and then shall deliver for our future.
Let us hold fast with an attitude of gratitude by
Staying on the path to grow our greatest future.

BKH 2021

If Not Now?

When should all wars stop,
    If not now?
When should plundering stop,
    If not now?
When should world religions co-exist,
    If not now?
When should peace prevail,
    If not now?
When should love triumph over hate,
    If not now?
When should starvation stop,
    If not now?
When should child abuse stop,
    If not now?
When should angels stop crying,
    If not now?
When should we take care of our health,
    If not now?
When should light outshine darkness,
    If not now?

BKH 2020

Tinker At Your Own Peril

Never fear freedom but do face the chase.
Interfere not with genuine problem solvers.
Criticize only if you have the heart to help.
Believe that a mess made can still be fixed.
Face any sadness that feels overwhelming.
Don't do anything wrong to do something right.
Avoid endorsing the disintegration of goodness.
Never obstruct genuine preservers of life.
Makers of their own magic will be movers.
Seek out those having the will to be builders.
Be not drawn in by enchanting human fakers.
And don't encourage any rumor mongers.
Support those who contribute to a better world.
Let go where needed and get on with living.
The keystone of truth supports a sound world.
Have a bias for action that is constructive.

Dancing with the devil is a dead-end road.
As a student, always be a teacher too.
Hold on to what matters and let go of the past!
Only you can truly rescue you from yourself.
Daily, fireproof all that matters most to you.
Take the time to do more when it's needed.
Act on your imagination in order to bear fruit.
Don't handcuff yourself to any falsehoods.
It's normal for us to hunger for togetherness.
Be at the ready to take a righteous stand.
Compassion and conviction grow courage.
Know what you stand for and commit to it.
Fear not what is daunting; take that first step.
If you had only today, make the most of it.
Move forward with passion and purpose.
And pledge yourself to right human relations.

BKH 2021

Imagine!

Imagine, be not charmed by any known deceiver.
Imagine, if you had everything, would it be enough?
Imagine, that we never give up on our dreams.
Imagine, a humble life will nurture a better you.

Imagine, choices made which bring harm to no one.
Imagine, that one's better nature deserves to blossom.
Imagine, if love finally stops all hate in its tracks.
Imagine, scars, as skeletons on our soul, are discharged.

Imagine, the world needs our constructive contributions.
Imagine, shedding anything that ever held us back.
Imagine, a lush moonlit night and that all was right.
Imagine, never taking for granted any day in one's life.

Imagine, the gift of inspiration that produces good deeds.
Imagine, today, that peace can prevail in this world of ours.
Imagine, choosing to embrace right human relations.
Imagine, intentional action on our part to make it so.

BKH 2021

Be Who You Are

As a child I was told,
"Honesty builds character."
Over the years I learned
That it is an important trait.
To be who you are is to
Always be true to yourself.
Honesty provides health
For our solid soul growth.
To be true to oneself is to
Accept who we really are.
Afterall, we have to live in
This life never fearing a mirror.
Doing it day in and day out
Allows one to be ok with oneself.
Well, why wouldn't we, really?

BKH 2021

My Soul Song

Those lullabies sung to me
Soothed my new born soul.
Take two came as a toddler
And dreaming of what's next?
In my youth came an awakening
That would change my life.
Two near-death experiences
Revealed how precarious life can be.
My growing soul song was always
Heard during this thing called life.
My pathway forward was fitting
For a guy known to be so spirited.
Some bells tolling seem to rale
Against me when least expected.
A growing spirit will be challenged
And so, my soul song remains fluid.
Fears faced become neutralized
By enthusiastic spiritual growth.
Day by day; even year by year,
Solace of my soul song is wanted.
May it be for many, many eons
As my glow grows in light and love.

BKH 2021

Wealth Comes In Many Forms

Committing to do what's best for my health
Allowing change a chance to be inspirational
Reserving the choice to think for myself
Facing any fear in pursuit of resolution
Using common sense will serve me well
Doing the right thing, even when no one is looking
Congregating with positive, likeminded people
Experiencing love through give and take
Being in my core, righteous in thought and deeds
Striving to excel at my human evolution
Having passion for purposeful living
Learning that kind words have healing power
Acknowledging dreams realized move me forward
Believing truly that right does make might
Nurturing my soul in a faithful way for spiritual growth
Battling darkness with constant spiritual light
Regarding courage, speaking truth to power
Living fully with an attitude of gratitude
Knowing wealth comes in many forms

BKH 2021

A Leap Of Faith

Relish what warms your heart
During each and every new start.
Never allow yourself to be late
As you navigate to overcome hate.
If growing should require going,
What seeds of life are you sowing?
When traveling a road that long,
Sing about life, your engaging song.
For all, it's always ok to be bold
As you find purpose beyond the fold.

Be not a fate fearer on this day
When keeping obstructors at bay.
Strengthened by our inner voice,
We form good habits through choice.
A heart shackled because of fear
Is absolutely nothing to hold dear.
A leap of faith made by we the daring
Will be fortified through genuine caring.
As we should daily rise above the fray,
It requires leaving each by-gone day.

BKH 2021

My Drum Beat

My drum beat can be yours too
By getting after what is your due.

I do wield a sharp writing sword
Of wisdom you can turn toward.
If necessary, to validate your worth,
Travel to the ends of this earth.

My drum beat can be yours too
By getting after what is your due.

For spiritual seeds we should sow,
There'll be life struggles we know.
Positive adapting begets us growing,
And most can see our auras glowing.

My drum beat can be yours too
By getting after what is your due.

It's how we live that truly matters.
And nothing free is served on platters.
Be beckoned by the righteous brave
And never, ever, be anyone's slave.

My drum beat can be yours too
By getting after what is your due.

It's caring power by me and you
That grows heavenly wealth we accrue.
I suggest we do more than dream,
And swear loyalty to the life stream.

My drum beat can be yours too
By getting after what is your due.

BKH 2021

Find Your Way

Even when thought lost,
You can find your way.
A heart filled with love knows
You can find your way.
Go to where you are wanted.
You can find your way.
Use a lighthouse beacon;
You can find your way.
At whatever pace you choose,
You can find your way.
If you never give up
You can find your way.
Hold on if touched by pain;
You can find your way.
Take one step then take two;
You can find your way.
Life is not always easy but
You can find your way.
Don't follow the pied piper;
You can find your way.
Make your plan then know
You can find your way.
Believe tomorrow will come;
You can find your way.
Don't ever give up because
You can find your way.

BKH 2021

I Know That

The sun will rise every day.
"I know that."
The sky is blue.
"I know that."
You are our firstborn child.
"I know that."
It's time to eat.
"I know that."
It's time to go to bed.
"I know that."
You can ask for help.
"I know that."

BKH 2021

I walked at 10 months old
and was fiercely independent.
Between 2 and 3 years old I
started saying "I know that" to my
parents when they would ask me
a question or told me most anything.
They found it amusing, as I was serious.

Be A World Ambassador

Keep rage in a cage until reason prevails.
Each of us should be a World Ambassador.
Ambassadors must make time for real action.
Shine a light on what's wrong and what is right,
As an Ambassador for right human relations.
Who is watching this troubled world of ours?
Whether or not you realize it, individual effort
Is recorded by those Universal recordkeepers.

It is the responsibility of all Ambassadors
To use their voice for humanitarian reasons.
A true World Ambassador must be present
With passion for doing what is universally right.
Ambassadors always need to be bravely visible
And should only be faithful to their moral duty.
We can offer solutions; Ambassadors must act.
Who are you and what are you doing each day?

Does our world deserve a second chance?
There are real arguments for yes and for no.
If it be no, then make the most of each day.
If yes, then what are we doing daily to finally
Contribute as individual World Ambassadors?
Kind voices and beneficial choices will help us.
The world urgently needs a course correction.
We succeed by holding to our moral compasses.

BKH 2020

Do You Understand

Do you understand...
You go nowhere without a plan.
Do you understand...
Freedom of choice requires responsibility.
Do you understand...
It's best to be the captain of your own ship.
Do you understand...
Righteous vision produces real change.
Do you understand...
You are a student and a teacher too.
Do you understand...
Deeds speak louder than words.
Do you understand...
The ultimate is leaving a legacy that lives on.
Do you understand...
Compassion is an expression of love.
Do you understand...
Make a difference where you can.
Do you understand...
True worth is in the growth of your spirit.
Do you understand...
Relief comes from belief in the beyond.
Do you understand...
Earth is only a springboard to eternity.

BKH 1984

When The Rose Fades

Our seasons swiftly come and go.
We travel life's roads seeking, ever
Seeking, the sense of our purpose for being.
Like a rose's many transformations,
Growth is gained by nurturing, labor and love.
When we are a rose in full bloom,
Often, it is too late in life.
Recognition of our wondrous beauty
And celebration of life,
Strengthens and encourages each change.
When the rose fades,
What remains is a mirror of ourselves;
Growth, transformation, and greater love.
Find comfort during this transition
As you seek your life anew.

BKH 2000

This poem became the title of Brion's first book of poetry which can be purchased at his website: www.BrionKHanks-Poetry.com.

The Human Hero Known As Empathy

The human gut feeling we experience
Surely is a hero known as empathy.
Tears shed upon hearing a sad tale
Do demonstrate one's empathy.
Pain acknowledged on a friend's face
Illustrates that our empathy is alive.
A child with an arm around a buddy
Validates youthful human empathy.

Wickedness will beget consequences
That could exclude genuine empathy.
Any empathy deniers may be a casualty
That makes them less than fully human.
For the sake of you and whomever,
Keep empathy close to your heart
As the hallmark of real caring power.
To lose empathy is to be inhuman.
Why would we? Really, why would we?

All doers of evil, at a minimum,
Deserve to know karmic justice.
It's ok to be wary of the rude who are
Unwilling to graciously know empathy.
The Amygdala must be protected
Because it is our empathy originator.
Empathy, the human hero that we
All need, is best held near and dear.
To lose empathy is to be inhuman.
Why would we? Really, why would we?

BKH 2021

Push Back The Darkness

We can increase light and push back the darkness by:

Acknowledging the need to love and be loved
Planned and random acts of kindness
Truly listening
Giving a smile
Planting a tree
Writing a poem
Hugging a friend
Protecting nature
Nurturing children
Speaking the truth
Making a difference
Holding our heads high
Thinking good thoughts
Imparting what we learn
Simply caring and sharing
Doing rather than just talking
Foregoing fame for influence
Committing to self-improvement
Being grateful for what we have
Striving to give more than we get
Producing more than we consume
Giving for the joy of the experience
Reaching out a hand to the helpless
Believing that balance brings beauty
Living our lives with a positive purpose
Knowing that struggle enhances growth
Unconditionally, laboring with love in our hearts
Realizing that wisdom is the right use of knowledge
Recognizing our Creator as the First Principle in all things

BKH 1984

Epilogue

Nearly fifty years of writing have gone into this book of poetry and prose. In a way, I have laid myself bare and given you the opportunity to share in this life of mine.

It is a fact; life is not always smooth and upbeat. We go through trials and tribulations, experiencing good and bad times that were both happy and sad. I accept it all as a part of growing my body, mind and spirit.

Always, I have utilized passion and purpose to move myself forward while striving mightily to make a difference along my life journey, as a means to know success in this life. Please do the same.

To be the change we want is empowering and contagious in a righteous way. Let's create life building blocks that are suitable, adaptable and sustainable.

Expectations, great and positive expectations for our world that desperately needs it, shall realize success through human empathy. May we look backward to learn but forward to discern we can be open to and achieve waves of peace and prosperity! Who can make it happen? Ah, each of us must do our part.

We all go through "endings." And we are reaching the end of the tales of this traveler. At least for now. Afterall, any end is but a new beginning... And do remember, tomorrow is a new day! *Strive on!!*

Light and love,
Brion K Hanks 2021

Postscript

Making A Difference

The Starfish Story

Once there was a great storm that washed thousands of starfish to the high tide line. As an old man walked along the beach he observed a young boy picking up starfish and quickly returning them to the sea. Picking up starfish and returning them to the sea.

The man approached the boy and said, "What are you doing? The sun is rapidly rising. What difference does it make? They are all going to die anyway?"

As the boy rose from picking up another starfish he said, "What difference does it make? It will make a difference to this one!"

The boy then returned that starfish to the sea. And, as best he could, made a difference one starfish at a time.

Think on this. It is suggested we all practice that boy's example. We can, in a mere moment, make a difference when we least expect it. Be open to and patience with every chance you are given to do so.

BKH 2021

www.ingramcontent.com/pod-product-compliance
Lightning Source LLC
Chambersburg PA
CBHW071325120626
46546CB00002B/451